TWICE VIOLATED

New Hope for the Victims of Criminal Violence

Robert C. Sullivan

VANTAGE PRESS
New York / Los Angeles / Chicago

Dedicated to the Washington State Patrol, where it all started upon the hit-and-run, line-of-duty death of one of its members, and to all other silent victims of criminal violence.

FIRST EDITION

Published by Vantage Press, Inc.
516 West 34th Street, New York, New York 10001

Manufactured in the United States of America
ISBN: 0-533-07799-0

Library of Congress Catalog Card No.: 87-90284

Contents

Graphs and Charts		v
Forweward		vii
Preface		xi
1.	Genesis	1
2.	The Very Early Years	11
3.	Death on Neptune Avenue	26
4.	The Background Setting	43
5.	The Disquiet Evidence	55
6.	Mastering the Fundamentals	69
7.	The Unbelievable Silence	89
8.	The Men in Blue	113
9.	A New Access Strategy	126
10.	The Eureka Discovery	150
11.	Heroes for the Prosecution	162
12.	Seeking a Solution	175
13.	A Sham	196
14.	Epilogue	209
15.	Sources of Appeal	218
	Bibliography	221

GRAPHS AND CHARTS

Crime Laboratory Organization Chart

Experts by Default

Subjective Probability for Forensic Effectiveness

Pro-Active Interactive Criminalistics Experts

Operational Effectiveness-OE Factor-Developed

FOREWORD

A report card produced by the criminal justice system in these United States:

Recent crime statistics indicate that there have been over 35 million crimes reported to the police in one year.

Within these fifty states, 25 percent of the nation's households were touched by crimes of violence or theft.

These statistics indicate that there have been over 5.5 million victims of criminal violence each year.

These numbers indicate that one out of every 133 Americans will become a murder victim (1:133) and one out of each twelve women will be a rape victim (1:12).

The National Crime Prevention Council states that violent crime is one hundred times more likely to strike than pneumonia, death, or auto accident. Violent crime is expected to strike eight times more than heart disease and sixteen times more than death from cancer.

These numbers are growing at a rate of over 8 percent per year (1984 crime statistics).

If the above can be considered a typical crime record of many years standing, and with an equally well established criminal recidivism rate in excess of 80 percent, a life of crime does appear to be cost effective when one also considers the high number of crimes committed vs. the low individual conviction rate and that it is at least a 10 billion dollar a year industry. Crime in the United States is certainly a very successful growth industry.

These statistics never reflect the unnecessary suffering caused by these perpetrators to the original victims nor to successive victims of violent crimes when these culprits are permitted to avoid detection in the first arrest instance, and they are then able to repeatedly strike again.

If the present criminal justice system, in which all of this has taken place, were a baseball team with this record, it would not be considered a serious applicant for even the bush leagues.

Our national life is ended as soon as it has lost the power of noble anger. When it paints over and apologizes for its pitiful criminalities and endures its false weights and adulterated food, dares not decide practically between good and evil and can neither honor the one nor smite the other, but sneers at the good as if it were hidden evil and consoles the evil with pious sympathy, the end is come.

—John Ruskin

Let justice be done—even though the heavens fall.
—William Watson, over the threshold to "Old Baily" Courthouse, London, England

PREFACE

A life that is unexamined is not worth living.

—Plato's Dialogue
Apology, line 38

Throughout this country our advocatory system of law (as contained in the criminal justice system) requires that the state prove that the accused in a criminal trial is guilty of the offense charged "beyond a reasonable doubt" and that such final decisions of fact be made only by a jury of one's peers. In all too many cases, however, the victims of criminal violence never do get their day in court because of a systematic, institutionalized inflexibility in criminal case analyses within many of the nation's crime laboratories. This has developed because there has been a technical mismatch among the prosecution "experts," who are charged with serving these victims, and all too few of these "experts" really care for it to be otherwise.

The victims of criminal violence (both primary and secondary) are powerless, helpless, and voiceless because they are disassociated with each other in time, place, and circumstances and because there is *no militant constituency* to plead their cases before any elected governing body—be it at the local, state, or federal level—when the present criminal justice system fails to adequately meet their personal needs at trail. This is most evident and devastating when a homicide or other felony occurs and the state's technical expert examiners confine themselves only to observations, tests, and conclusions that are totally objective and free of all error regardless of the crime, type of evidence received from a crime scene, or other mitigating circumstances. The technical test procedures that are required to arrive at any of these decisions are initially difficult to comprehend but with time and repetition they do become comfortable routines and the profession demands that the results must be conclusive before any written report is sent to court.

Once these decisions have been made in the local crime laboratory there is no appeal process to reconsider the criminal evidence that is rejected by these prosecution experts when they work in such self-protective modes. Since their opaque reports abound in rhetoric (pro forma utterances) and lack critical realism, there are few attempts to meet the victims of criminal violence at their points of need and this creates a gross miscarriage of justice. (If any retail outlet were as deaf, dumb, blind, and anemic as the present criminal justice system, it would be short-lived.)

In the interest of substantive justice for victims, the prosecution experts do grave disservice to their legal and moral responsibilities when they fail to consider the real implications in less than perfect criminal evidence that does so often come to their attention. There seems to be *no discontent* that more could be done with the inherent, genuine voids we are forced to work with. As experts for the nation's criminal courts, they should be more "mission capable" and take control, but instead they have become slaves to the very forces they should dominate. These experts have allowed modern technology and their unhealthy professional tidiness to shape their goals. They have failed to realize the hidden and wasted potential in the criminal evidence that they are given to examine and that their decisions in each of these cases are significant. They have become firemen who will not fight the difficult fires because "they might get hurt"; combat soldiers who are rarely awarded medals for valor in combat; astronauts who refuse to accept the inherent risks of their profession. These experts have forgotten that the victims of criminal violence and their desperate needs are the central reason for these crime laboratories to exist. These experts must not place their career concerns above their consciences if these victims are to be properly served. If the present condition continues, society will find that the most desirable future will become the least likely, while the most likely future will become the least desirable.

The deplorable situations illustrated in the following pages are today's reality in our present criminal justice system—namely, the absolute absurdities in logic by denying inductive reasoning and the resulting more subtle, collision avoidances by these experts, at a criminal trial regardless of the costs to the victims of criminal violence. This has been conveniently accomplished by failing to review the status quo in criminal investigations and failing to give any recognition to the existence of secondary circumstantial evidence. This is incomplete circumstantial evidence that is somewhat less than the very best, that is present in the vast majority of criminal cases being submitted by the police to local crime laboratories. This failure to alert the local prosecutors and trial juries to this type of incomplete evidence is an inappropriate response to the needs of the crime victims by the experts for the prosecution. Certainly there is little credit due to the individual expert who will only render an opinion, interpreting only the circumstantial evidence that is of the very best quality (primary circumstantial evidence), that which contains no technical imperfections and ignoring all other evidence that does not reach this utopian level of credibility. It will be demonstrated that these professional chemists are occupationally disabled when working in criminalistics. They, like the atheist, will not take "know" for an answer.

This has developed because the more than two hundred crime laboratories in the nation are almost totally decentralized, with few technically competent senior police officials to coordinate the activities of their subunits. There are no oversight committees nor government-like accounting offices (GAO) that require any accountability to any elected or appointed officials and these senior police authorities have no meaningful administrative controls to monitor the technical activities of their own crime laboratories. (The available statistics are totally self-serving and reflect only to a small degree the efficiency of these units, never their effectiveness.) There has also been a mismatch in the selection and employment of professional chemists who demand for their casework analyses, deductive, objective decision matrixes, fixed determinations, and elaborate instrumentation systems. The process allows only minimum exposure to any risks, since "the expert analysts" insist on very high "benchmark" decision-making techniques and use only linear and deductive thinking processes even though the vast majority of criminal cases are, by their very nature, imperfect. The victims of criminal violence never become aware that their individual cases will not receive the vigorous criminal prosecution they deserve unless their cases are technically perfect. These victims never become aware of this second violation of their civil rights and this is a hidden price that is never seriously considered by the establishment. The criminal element has become aware that under the present circumstances the odds greatly favor their escaping full accountability for their individual crimes against others. As long as the criminal justice system is most concerned with technically perfect trials, criminals will continue to be set free, if apprehended at all. If criminals know that they can act with relative impunity and the citizens lose faith in the system, it will collapse due to its lack of response to society's needs. Presently, the criminal justice system is a monopoly and a self-reinforcing disaster.

Little attention is given to the needs of the victims of criminal violence or to the inductive use of the internal order, the predisposition as well as the predicatability in criminal evidence that is known to exist in nature—or in the subsequent, unexpected "happy events" (grim realism) that regularly appear in so many criminal cases. The traditionalism of the professional chemist rejects the fortuitous combinations of circumstances, as well as the use of common sense, logical consistencies, critical connections, cause and effect, statistical representative sampling techniques, inventive syntheses, the reasonableness of penetrating observations, and the whisperings of conscience—not to mention the plausible, persuasive intuitive probability which grows from the education, training, and experience of an authentic expert criminalist, who is considered an expert in scientific jurisprudence.

The predictabilities of "the smoking gun" are ignored by these chemists, as are the logical assumptions and implications present in most criminal evidence, and the fact that the final, binding decisions in all criminal cases are meant to be made by our elected prosecutors or trial juries—not in a crime laboratory. We fail to realize that the victims of criminal violence have the same right to a meaningful defense of their civil rights as any defendant and that we criminalists are the state's experts in our advocatory system of justice and therefore, must be proactive in the victim's defense and interactive with the criminal evidence even though it is less then perfect, incomplete, or less than the very best. We must not passively abandon our chosen responsibilities to the victims of criminal violence by failing to see the value[1] in the circumstantial evidence that is to be found in most criminal cases.

A new decision matrix and monitoring system has been developed, calling for the use of analytical, inductive, intuitive probability that will materially assist the authentic criminalist to uncover the hidden agendas present in the vast majority of criminal cases. If criminalists are the advocates of justice they are supposed to be, the mere presentation of this incomplete evidence to the presecutor and/or to the trial jury does not require overwhelming evidence or indubitable proofs. Such information does not automatically turn uncertainty into certainty, but does fulfill our responsibilities and takes us into personal involvement with the victims. In using the suggested mechanism of inductive probability as a realistic strategy we discretely introduce a new clause for wider jury consideration allowing the inherent ability in the imperfect evidence to "speak" if given the opportunity in a court of criminal law. We suggest this new critical access system in the name of common sense, law, social justice, and equity, and believe that society is committing suicide if such measures are not used. The proposed scheme is an effort for large scale repair of the basic infrastructure in law enforcement's technical units. As experts for the prosecution, we must not deny our consciences nor give control of them to senior bureaucrats. Our opinions must be expressed. As Thoreau has clearly asked, "Why, then, has every man been given a conscience?"

These pages describe one person's struggle against the present system. They show the consequences suffered when one attempts to redirect errant activities from the inside and is seen as a "whistleblower" by bureaucrats who are too content with their present comfortable system to care about the victims they are paid to serve. Authentic criminalists are a vital part of a system (police, crime laboratory, prosecutor) that should be mutually cooperative. Crime laboratories need to supply prosecutors with all the information necessary to support charges against identified defendants. If any one of these parts fails in its assigned duties, the victims are violated a second time by the very forces that are supposed to assist them.

Is there anyone else out there who cares? In time, you or a loved one may need these services but it will be too late to change the system and your needs will also go unanswered. In every instance that a perpetrator is not apprehended because these "experts" have failed to perform their duties, the culprit is free to again commit another atrocity and create more innocent victims. If you are at all concerned, please ride along with me and examine this unenviable situation.

MEANINGFUL DISCLOSURES

1. Value is an individual, subjective judgment that knows that any incomplete evidence is less than the very best, less than what you would like to work with but that there often is a *comprehensible reality*, a sense of meaningful significance in the incomplete evidence that is present in many imperfect criminal cases. This value must not remain a wasted potential, silent, (if we as experts for the criminal courts are to "go to ground" and reveal the hidden agendas in the evidence) due to our inability to articulate its existence to the criminal courts. It is for others to judge (prosecutors, grand juries, trial juries, and the criminal courts) as to the efficacy of our findings. Only by expressing these intangible "experiences of value" can there be a reality of conscience, of duty, and of our responsibilities to the victims of criminal violence. The recognition *and* expression of this valued intangible depends on our acknowledgment that there does exist a higher law than that which is expressed in any statute because there does exist a philosophy in life higher than Secular Humanism.

The analysts who do acknowledge that in the vast majority of criminal cases, the inevitable voids that do exist can be "filled" by using value judgments are effectively responding to this intangible conviction and are proactive experts in defense of the victims of criminal violence.

Those prosecution analysts who consistently deny this premise, testify only on concrete, objective evidence when completeness and professional prestige is assured (ignoring the less than perfect criminal cases and the inherent professional risks involved) are passive defenders in our advocatory system of justice, and are failing in their duty to more meaningfully respond to the needs of these victims and are causing a calamity in society's search for justice. (See Chapter Eight and its footnote #2.)

Chapter 1

GENESIS

The essence of knowledge is, having it, to use it.

—William James

The time is late August, 1982, at about 6:30 P.M., as Bob Sullivan, a tall, middle-aged state employee steps into a white patrol car belonging to the Department of Public Safety, State of Arizona. He is the director of the State Crime Laboratory in Flagstaff, Arizona, and is heading home after a trying, bewildering day spent at State Patrol Headquarters. Unknowingly, he is beginning his last trip north, on the only highway heading north, out of the city of Phoenix, Arizona.

It has been a very hot day in more ways than one, he says to himelf as he takes hold of the hot steering wheel and drives out of the city, beginning the lonely trip north to Flagstaff, some three hours and 150 miles in distance. As he heads home, he looks out the windshield of this marked state vehicle with the "meatballs" prominently displayed on the outside of each front door (state seal of the Department of Public Safety, State of Arizona - DPS). Within his view is the severely cracked, foam rubber-protected dashboard that has gone as solid as steel, from too many weeks of this severe desert heat. "These cars sit in this heat so long that they age faster from the sun than from use," he mumbles to himself as he unbuttons his collar and tie and tries to vent his body heat from his coatless body, the suit coat having been tossed unceremoniously onto the rear seat of the car when the drivers' door was first opened. The car's large air conditioner gradually cools the interior of the car and his comfort level increases as he maneuvers the full-sized car through city traffic and leaves the populated areas and the "snow birds" behind. They sure are right, he muses to himself at the cliché he had first heard of in Tucson, as it runs through his whirling mind. "The best way to see Phoenix is in the rearview mirror." As the minutes pass, the traffic becomes lighter and the car increases speed. What a day and what a mess—this whole thing can't be happening in this day and age are the thoughts tumbling through his mind. Here I am a college professor at Northern Arizona University (NAU) and for the first time in my life, a director of a state crime laboratory.

As the sun starts to lose its control of the thermometer and the desert heat becomes a cooler breeze of air, he continues his quiet mental debate. They say you are what you want to be and they are so right especially in my case. I am doing what I always wanted to do and it sure has been interesting—everything in this job is different, almost everyday; Monday is totally different from Tuesday or Wednesday and once in a while you do contribute to getting the bad guys. It is not like being a bank teller—the faces all do change and become a big blur, but there is a real difference. It is the challenge—the knowing that I will be needed behind the real scenes to help put all those little pieces of information from a very untidy scene together. I will not have wasted my life watching people come and go. I'll have been part of it—really part of it.

These victims really do need someone to help them—they don't ask much really—but their need is so great and I am part of it. I am what I always wanted to be, a college professor and a crime laboratory director, but I am also becoming a whistle-blower or, at least, they think so.

A whistleblower? Is that what I am? For some reason the term whistleblower has always had a negative image for me, he continues in his silent reflections. A person who joins an organization and is allowed to go behind the scenes as a trusted employee, only to surface at some future time with a story to tell that embarrasses associates and the organization he was an integral part of for so long. A reformer perhaps? No! Just a sinner with a conscience.

Why me—Why me? was an echo that reverberated endlessly in his mind. I had a good job, doing what I wanted to do, being where I always wanted to be! Why jeopardize all that for people I'll never really know? I was told so long ago that the really smart people never get involved. "You'll never get any thanks or promotions for putting your neck on the block for these people," the said. "They'll be old news tomorrow and you'll still need a paycheck and friends and if you rock the boat, if you make waves, you'll lose both. Don't you realize how really small your boat is? Don't you know that to get along you have to go along? If it works, don't fix it—don't look for trouble," they said.

I wish I could forget. I really do, but there is something in these little anxieties inside me that keep gnawing at me. Too many people really need help and I am supposed to be out there helping them; that is what I am paid to do.

The car engine is almost turning over as fast as his mind is reflecting the day's experiences; certainly the bridges, the highway exits and entrances are passing unnoticed as the car mechanically stays on the roadway. Somewhere I recently read that for every fifty crimes reported to the police, there is only one conviction. That is a god-awful ratio, isn't it? His mind tumbles and gets confused with all the crosscurrents going through it. There was a time when I didn't have these responsibilities nor the expertise and really no authority . . . but the times have changed with the years and the problems, too. What was it that they used to say—"We don't get older, we just get better." I sure hope they're right; but what is "it" that will not go away? I can only describe it as a strong belief in individual responsibility that has grown

3

ever stronger in me with the passing years. Of course, a good job has to be done as often as possible but with the understanding that we never know it all or do things—anything—near perfectly. That sure rings a bell in my ear as if in a firehouse, and the signal for a five-alarm fire has just sounded.

That damnable situation today in Phoenix headquarters, the state of the rising sun, sure was an absolute farce! "Zero error," they said; I must maintain zero error "in all things, technical as well as administrative." What an incentive killer that is in anyone's hands. I wonder which is worse, this demand for "zero error" or the other ridiculous quote from my other boss—that I "must never allow any case to leave the crime laboratory unless it is proven beyond a scientific doubt." There was to be no room for mistakes or errors.[1] What a joke on the people trying to do a good job under realistic conditions. Only obedient angels could meet these standards. It really would be a bad joke except that through their words and actions they were absolutely serious in the establishment of this criteria.

"It will be a cold day in hell before any intelligent person takes the real responsibilties of this profession seriously under these conditions," I mused. Where is their obligation to the victims of these serious crimes? Where is their obligation to me as a mid-manager to lay that on me after the fact as an "unwritten policy" more than two years after they selected me for this job? I never, in my twenty-two years as a criminalist and supervisor, ever heard of such nonsense. Why don't they be more truthful and say that CYA is the real administrative policy and be done with it? I remembered that I never had confidence in anyone who refused to admit he had made mistakes of some type in his career. Admitting mistakes teaches humility and caution and any expert who doesn't have these qualities is a dangerous analyst because only the foolish and the dead never make mistakes.

I would never have moved from Seattle as bad as that situation was, had I known about this. Can they be serious? Don't they

4

realize that in equity, all DPS employees must then be meeting this same impossible level of performance? Oh yes, I remember, at that hearing when I objected to this unwritten policy, one of the board members said, "I see nothing wrong with zero error—we do it all the time with computers." The other two members of the board only smiled and by their silence gave approval. Everything went downhill after that, and predictably so. There was not going to be any critical policy review of my complaints because "the system" was thought to be working fine. No credibility was going to be given to the ancients who believed that "a life which is unexamined is not worth living."

I remember thinking that there had to be a sensible way out of this situation so I tried to continue to stay "in the system" and use the established departmental grievance procedure to vent my concern and obtain official determinations on these matters. It guaranteed me that "no disciplinary action would be taken against any employee who utilized the procedure." That turned out to be a joke, too. I thought I was dealing with sincere individuals or that, at least, I would meet someone in higher levels who would play the devil's advocate and see through all their hidden agendas and pure smoke, but no one did. Couldn't they see that this punishment is retaliation and this personal harassment and intimidation is against my refusal to withdraw that second technical publication? They knew when they hired me I had been professionally publishing for fifteen years. The powers that be couldn't have been more clear in their intent in that phone call from Phoenix headquarters—"If you refuse to withdraw that paper, we will do all in our power to stop you from publishing it."

Failing to have accomplished that, they sure pulled all the stops to punish me for that insubordination. They were forced to develop a set of phantom charges against me that would hide the hidden agenda they were really concerned with. In doing so, any academic freedom that did exist through my teaching and publishing at the university was badly compromised. I sure tried to explain to the Major that I firmly believed in the professional approach to such matters and did not want to wash our dirty linen in public either, and had no intention of doing so. Didn't he realize that discussing professional problems in professional peer-reviewed journals was not washing our dirty linen in public? I had gone to no newspapers here or in Seattle!

These were serious problems that had to be faced and not ignored if we professionals were going to help these victims of violent crimes at their point of need.[2] That is our job—that is what we are paid to do! That is our dignity. As criminalists and experts for the criminal courts, we are supposed to give our opinions to the criminal courts whenever it is reasonably possible to do so. Playing these games that have a high premium on "don't rock the boat" or following a policy of CYA (risk aversion and timidity) has no place for a professional court expert. Taking all that has happened into mind, not only were we not to wash our dirty linen in public, we were not going to be able to do it in private either, the victims be damned.

I had for many years digested and accepted these corporate values and now that I had managerial and academic responsibilities and was trying to break away from this heartless, inflexible, insensitive approach to case analyses and develop a more compassionate path—the system is trying to kill me professionally—the First Amendment be damned. They might just get away with it if no one understands, because I am, after all, an "employee at will" and have no rights. I am, and the many victims of criminal violence are, going to pay the price for their gross failure in policy making.

The desert air had cooled considerably by now, but the sole passenger had again become as warm as ever, even with the car air conditioner still on the high position. The steering wheel had cooled off, but he hadn't.

This driver continued to reminisce in an attempt to make some sense out of his recent and dreadful experiences. I never like whistleblowers as such unless, of course, serious circumstances forced these people to become rebels with a cause. In that case, conscience has to come first and you are forced to become an ethical resistor. Whistleblowers, it seems, are persons with a conscience who are caught between a rock and a hard place, with almost no place to go. They know the easy way out (to keep silent and avoid confrontations as often as possible) but refuse to take it, because of the seriousness of the situation. These problems that I have been facing cannot be ignored any longer, at least not by me. In my college days, great stress was placed on the fact that in reality we are not firemen, accountants, chemists, lawyers, managers, et cetera, but pilgrims, given a stewardship of responsibility. "Convictions of conscience cannot be repressed," it was said. "Utterances of conscience must be heard!"

Old Thomas Jefferson, in his letters of 1802, said it first and, perhaps, best of all time: "Man has no natural right in opposition to his social duties."

If the third president of the U.S. still lived, would he disagree that an authentic criminalist must speak the truth when he knows it, or failing to do so would be guilty of abdication of his responsibilities? I think not. The fight that has to be fought is a lonely fight, because all too often the subject matter is thought to be too complicated or too removed from the ordinary citizen for it to be understood by them except and until they too (or a loved one) become victims of criminal violence. Then they find that they too are really alone and it is too late to change the system.

Whistleblowers are proactive professionals who realize that we all are called to "fight the good fight" even to the point that we must absorb an avalanche of hatred from those whom we are fighting and from those citizens and peers who do not know or yet care about the down to earth reality of the situation. It must be equally obvious to any critical observer that the wimps of the world do rise to positions of authority by filling the vacuums of those departed decision makers who were caught making real decisions—doing their jobs in the system. Once in their new positions of power the nincompoops remain there by continuing to make few decisions—none of which are ever controversial; that has become their road to success—that is how they keep getting promoted and replace the real decision makers. As analysts, the decisions they make are made for the comfort of these experts, not that of the victims. There is something hollow and even petty in these analysts, I thought. This is what upset me in Seattle, having the expertise and capability but not yet the decision-making authority that I needed to live with myself, on a day-to-day basis. My frustrating six-year search for the needed answers started there in Seattle, with that hit and run, line of duty death of a Washington state trooper (WSP) in Mount Vernon. It was the very first case I had ever done, as the new chief criminalist for the patrol.

As with all cases I had ever done, there were great similarities and some dissimilarities with other cases. The milestone it represented to me was similar to the ones I faced in Arizona and had faced many years before while in the New York City Crime Laboratory (NYCPD). Meaningful decision making had been eluding me for too many years. There, in Washington State, I was faced with another serious case and I still was not fully prepared for it! Why not? Had I not testified at the criminal trial in Mount Vernon professionally and done the best that could be done? Yes indeed. It was not until after the reduced verdict that I knew that my testimony again had been inadequate. My testimony should have been stronger—but how?

Something more forceful could have helped the prosecution secure the higher verdict of vehicular homicide if I had only been not more prepared, but better prepared. I had again waited too long to solve the problem that I knew existed from almost my earliest days in New York. I sure asked a lot of questions back then, but the rational answers that were freely given left me unsatisfied, still hungry. The answers given were not enough then and became totally inadequate as the years passed. It takes time for all the ideas, standards, methods, formulas, and wooden rules to be really digested, and then mentally assimilated. It is much like a cow regurgitating its cud. There is an integration process and it all takes time to surface and now the ticking time bomb has exploded in a way I could never have seen.

Of course, it wasn't always that way. I had all the answers in the beginning and only with time did the old truth come to mind: Too soon we grow old; too late we grow smart!

Maybe it is not too late, if I can be sure, really sure, of my facts and how it all started back then. Why have I been forced to travel this road when I am sure it could have been different and certainly a safer and easier life, if only fair comments had been considered on the real important issues too long kept taboo; if only I had the real answers back then in 1957 when it all started as I began my career in the New York City Police Department (NYCPD).

The white car traveling north on that almost deserted highway in central Arizona is an inert object clicking off the miles in response to the actions of its pondering driver. The sole occupant is mentally traveling faster and farther than the car in time and space.

MEANINGFUL DISCLOSURES

1. Categorical certitude; the application of the scientific method with nothing less than complete physical verification (empiricism) but with complete indifference to the less than perfect but incriminating evidence (artifacts) so often found in criminal cases. Little consideration is given to the ethical truth substantiated in so many of these cases. The ignored evidence then becomes "inadmissible" to a court of law by default. It is the processing

of just such "incomplete evidence" that the crime laboratory system was created as opposed to a standard chemical testing laboratory. Trial juries do not need experts to tell them what is obvious or what is reasonable to the ordinary citizen. The exclusion of this most basic rationale is the chief deficiency, a flaw built into the system by the mind set of its inventors. It is difficult to be fair to these chemists and laboratory managers who adhere to this philosophy considering the devastation the present system continues to produce following the stated policies.

2. See Chapter Fourteen for a specific instance when this policy was carried out to its fullest extent.

Chapter 2

THE VERY EARLY YEARS

Private interests must not be put in opposition to the public good.
—John Quincy Adams,
Embargo Bill 1807

As the white car continued its upward journey north, gradually climbing the winding roads that hugged the mountains' sides, the driver could experience nature's wonders in the ever deepening valleys below. The car was at times straining to reach the seven thousand foot plateau and the beautiful tree line that drastically separated the lower hot desert from the lush growth of evergreens in the northern part of the state of Arizona. Our driver automatically turned on the car radio to the police channel to hear the Flagstaff dispatcher, but he was oblivious to its chatter. For him the darkening, lonely road was an endless, twisting ribbon. It lay before him as this familiar journey repeated itself. We had nothing like these open spaces in New York, he thought to himself as he became lost in thought, again reflecting on his earlier career that had such a long term effect on him.

After graduating from Iona College and having read interesting items about the New York City Police Crime Laboratory, I learned that it was then the policy of the NYCPD that every person assigned to their crime laboratory, with very few exceptions, had to first qualify as a police officer; only two civilians were on the staff out of over one hundred assigned personnel. I took and passed the required civil service test and in time was appointed to the nine-month police academy recruit training program. The training period passed quickly and then, with academic police training behind me, I graduated and was assigned to an active police precinct before any transfers to other assignments were permitted. 'You have to get your feet wet,' I was often told, 'before anyone is allowed to look at you.' The PRU-I's (Personal Record Unit form #1) were useless until you were considered 'street smart' to some degree and had passed at least the first field evaulation in an active house. I was to learn firsthand while 'on patrol' what it is like to be New York's Finest.

Perhaps it began in that early training period, the character building and experience period that was to reflect itself so often in the future, I thought as I moved about in the speeding white car, its lights now reflecting the endless dashes of the broken traffic lines. Where else could a person better start a career in criminalistics than in the biggest police department then existing (sixteen thousand strong and it was to grow to over twenty-nine thousand during my career) and the best crime laboratory available. *Don't the biggest and the best go together*, I laughingly said to myself.

I do remember, quite clearly, that midnight to eight tour in uniform, in that busy Manhattan North Precinct. I can still hear that woman screaming at me as she ran towards me in her nightclothes. It was my first police action and she was terrified. Between gulps of air, she quickly told me that her apartment was then being burglarized. She had awoken to a noise in the front of the apartment and upon going into the front room, she confronted a strange man emptying her purse onto the living room table. He tried to subdue her and in the struggle raised a hammer to hit her as she escaped his grasp and bolted for the door. The situation, as it presented itself to me, required me to immediately make several decisions. Was I to immediately aid this woman and try to apprehend the thief or go to the police call box at the corner, some distance away and call for assistance? Who but I

12

was to say which option was the more correct? Both were acceptable actions and well within proper police procedure. The latter choice was, of course, the safest action to take. Personal longevity was assured in direct proportion to the safety measures taken to assure that longevity! The former places the officer in jeopardy—but with a decent chance to catch the thief, thus doing his job! I thought to myself as these options became apparent I either wear the badge and take pride in it or take it off and stop pretending I am something I am not! With all the noise out front and with many seconds already spent, certainly the thief was not going to stay around long. With the woman behind me yelling directions, I rushed and went down through an open basement corridor which lead to the rear of the building complex. No one had come out the front door as I approached and passed the front of the building; he either went up and over the rooftops or out the back fire escape from which he came. A gamble at best to be sure and I chose the alternative he seemed to know best—go out the way he came in! As I ran through the narrow corridor towards the rear courtyard, I had the presence of mind to smash the last three light bulbs before entering the expected darkened, backyard area. I didn't want my silhouette outlined against a bright background as I advanced into what was a dangerous and darkened area. Nothing of any consequence was to happen that night because (as I was to learn upon returning to the same location in daylight) there were at least a dozen exits from the courtyard area that allowed any thief to exit to the next street. The situation, among others, was a learning process. The police academy from which I had so recently come had the motto "Enter to learn—leave to serve," and I was doing just that, learning to serve. This first incident, as I review the scene now, set up a sequence of actions or patterns that in my professional future might not have developed or been available under any other circumstnaces. These situations illustrated the need and subsequent ability to accept or reject professional responsibility; to make the nonself-serving, the right, decisions under stress; to become aware and understand similar circumstances that others would face in the future. It is far too easy to criticize any police action unless you have experienced such episodes, too. That man from Missouri sure had it right—"If you can't stand the heat, stay out of the kitchen." Another old saying had a lot of truth in it too: "You are supposed to flower where you are planted." However, no one can do that if they ignore their present responsibilities. After all, that is exactly what this life is all about!

My career in criminalistics (scientific jurisprudence—a technical expert to the criminal courts)[1] began after "signing the book," having successfully passed the required one year probationary period with some field experience in a line precinct and then being transferred to the crime laboratory. This was my first opportunity to begin associating with "the real professionals" in criminalistics. Being young, receptive, and in awe of my surroundings, I tried to absorb the mountains of technical information from men like Charlie O'Hara, but without any of the inductive reasoning or even an awareness of the collateral responsibilities lingering there. I, of course, did not have then the in-depth technical knowledge, the maturity, the supervisory or subsequent managerial responsibilities I was to gain in future years. These voids would be filled in as the years advanced, as assignments changed, awards and promotions were granted and accepted.

The new profession I was entering was a specialty within police work. Through advanced education in the physical sciences, on-the-job training, and ever increasing case experiences over a period of years, you become a criminal court expert in one or more areas of specialization. As such, such individuals become experts for the criminal courts, a legal qualification obtained each time a "completed" written analysis was submitted and accepted in a court of law. This routinely happened several thousand times over the course of one's career. Very few times would any defense attorney attempt to challenge the analysis with

14

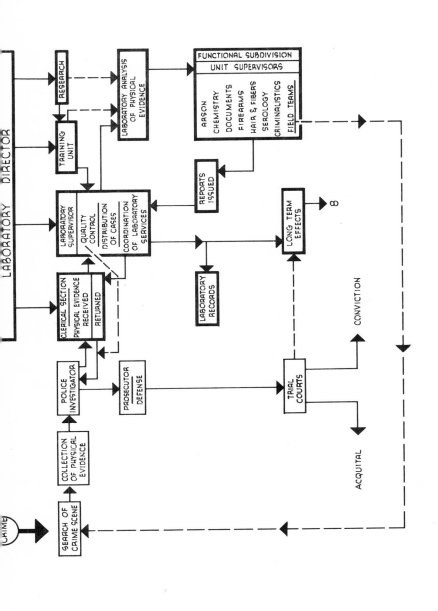

another opposing defense expert. Very few defense experts had the extensive background qualifications that a criminalist obtained from exposure to numerous situations. As time passed, one's reputation became established and fewer actual court appearances became necessary.

As an expert for the criminal courts, the individual was usually paid 10 to 15 percent more salary at each promotional level than his counterpart in a similar civil service level. The technical knowledge required at each level was the same, but each criminalistic analysis was more tedious (less routine) and the analyst could be required to testify to each of his analyses in a court of law and undergo cross-examination by the defense attorney. The added complexities of always working with small, irreplaceable, contaminated "unknown" evidence samples warranted a higher pay scale and it became a generally accepted practice.

As a court expert, one is exempt from the requirements of the hear-say rule in a court of criminal law. Under this legal exception a court recognized expert may give his opinion to the court with all parties being fully aware that the analyst was never at the crime scene at the time of occurrence. In rendering this expert opinion such testimony need not have the elevated level of total certainty before the court will allow such opinions to be given to a jury.[2] A criminal court expert can be anyone (medical doctor, an auto mechanic, a carpenter, a psychologist, et cetera) having specialized knowledge of any subject in which the court has a need during any trial.

My first learning experience in the crime laboratory was to begin with the assignment, after some orientation, to the crime scene field team.[3] It was a position I was to hold, in increasing degrees, for the next four years. As a new member of the crime laboratory, I spent the first several months on days alternating between working as a third wheel of a two-man crime scene response team and learning from (not working with, but watching) the various specialists performing their analyses on actual cases. This was a normal mix for an in-house training program when starting a new employee on the road to becoming a criminalist. Under these circumstances a new analyst began to learn, as a generalist, the internal coordinated functions of the various sections he would represent at a crime scene. Specific knowledge had to be absorbed as to what type of evidence each section actually worked on and the unit's limitations. This dual exposure not only permitted the transfer of a great deal of knowledge in the shortest amount of time, but mixed the application of academic case analyses with practical field application of the specifices learned. This type of in-house training made the supervised learning process very meaningful while waiting for a request for technical assistance at a crime scene where this newly acquired knowledge could be put to practical use under close supervision.

When working with "the teams," an attitude of "watch and learn" and "ask any questions you want after doing what you are directed to do" at the crime scene was a closely held motto. Depending on the individual's learning abilities, which was estimated from what questions were asked or not asked and actual crime scene performance, which materially demonstrated the level of comprehension, the person remained "the third wheel" for an undetermined period of time. As this exciting learning period passed, and with some agitation, one gradually started to respond alone to minor crime scenes regardless of the team caseload.

In New York, Monday mornings were always very busy, as the weekend always produced a backlog of low-priority cases when owners of businesses opened their stores for the day's customers only to find that their stores had been broken into during their absence. These numerous burglaries represented criminal cases that did not involve any type of personal injuries and, due to limited resources, the more serious cases involving personal assaults were tended to first.

The New York City Crime Laboratory, lovingly known as "the shop" by all the personnel who worked in it, was located on the second floor of the 84th Police Precinct building on Poplar Street in downtown Brooklyn. It was an old, nondescript building, four stories high, poorly situated on a narrow, sun-starved street. The precinct was poorly situated for the many different functions it was forced to perform. As a precinct, it was situated there with its uniformed force of line officers. The county homicide squad was situated there, as was the bomb squad and the crime laboratory. All of these independent units competed for room—to work and to park their cars. A narrow but busy one-way street, formed in almost a complete circle, went around the only access route that led to the stationhouse. If there were ever a fire, no fire truck could ever get near the building because the various police cars, line, and staff units, had to be double parked by their owners, only to be quickly replaced, as they left, by other cars on police business. At times the area seemed to be overwhelmed with activity.

On any normal Monday morning, it was the beginning of another week for me "on day duty." The telephones seemed to be ringing off the hook as I came within hearing distance of the front office. Usually this area is swarming with people, especially as the work shift is changing, the more important case assignments are discussed and given out, and the office staff attempts to take control of this organized confusion. With all these people milling about, some are supposedly helping the secretary to answer the phones. *So why are they still ringing?* I asked myself as I quickly passed through this busy front office. No matter. My job this day is to cover the minor cases obtained from the assignment sheets posted in the rear hallway. For a person of my low status, learning and coverage of these minor cases was the order of the day. Such an individual obtained their assignment and left quickly and unnoticed because all hell was breaking out for everybody else in "the shop." Those who really could teach and contribute to my learning process were themselves too busy to teach anyone anything today or on any Monday "day duty."

My first assignment was to handle an attempted burglary at Tiffany's Jewelry & Company, an exclusive jewelry store in midtown Manhattan.

After plowing through normal morning traffic, I arrived, solo, at Tiffany's on Fifth Avenue. Once again, as I frequently did, I met the familiar faces of newly assigned officers learning their specialties by the numbers, as I was doing. As I "bounced" from one minor scene to another, I would meet the same persons from burglary, photo, safe and loft squad, local detectives, or the youth squad, who were all new to their routines. The mutual inexperience showed. Many questions were asked and many phone calls made to the parent units after the completion of assignments. Besides giving you your next case, these "check-ins" helped assure that the jobs were being processed, that the new officer was following the correct procedures and filling out the right forms for his particular unit.

Upon arrival at Tiffany's, the same story was repeated to each arriving investigator by the uniformed patrolman guarding the premises. A male had been seen to throw a building brick at a display window, one of which was on either side of the front door to the store.

At about eight o'clock that Monday morning, just as I was coming on duty, a store security official (a rent-a-cop), was watching for approaching store personnel to check them in prior to the official daily opening of the store. He heard a loud thud and one of the alarms in the store was heard. Someone had thrown a building brick at one of the display windows, evidently in the desire to relieve the store of expensive rings and necklaces on display in the window. Unknown to the would be amateur thief, a less than careful inspection would have revealed a window pane four feet by three feet, but about one inch thick, certainly classified as bulletproof glass and obviously almost indestructible. A small but deep hole had been "drilled" into the window with almost no appearance of spiral fractures in the side from which the force was exerted. Due to the construction of the windowpane, the hole penetrated less than half the depth of the window. It was all too apparent why this group of investigators was sent from each responding office. In real terms this was not an attempted burglary by any stretch of the imagination, but a malicious mischief as a felony due only to the cost of a replacement window. An individual had been seen running "from the scene" by the store security officer. He had been arrested within a short distance after a chase by the store guard and given to a responding RMP (uniformed police unit in a radio motor patrol car) for transportation to the local precinct.

After these preliminaries and upon initial examination of the window (but prior to the mandatory latent print processing of the window), I seemed to notice something shining, almost flickering in the morning sunlight. Impressed in the hole of the window were eight or nine threads of material, each about two to three inches long; some appeared red and others yellow or gold in color. The training and theory I had received those first weeks with Charlie O'Hara were turning out to be true after all. Prior to extracting these fibers from the hole, I followed "the rules" and took pictures of the undisturbed scene with a ruler in place. (When the pictures were developed, the threads were not visible due to the damage and transparency of the glass. A hot spot also showed up in the photograph as a reflection of the sun on the window. It was indeed a learning process in which non-repeatable mistakes were accepted.)

Upon finishing my investigation, I too took my turn and waited on line to report my findings to the local precinct squad detective who had caught the case. It was the typical, no-nonsense shop. "Keep it short but give us the facts—fast" was the standard, unwritten, but often verbalized cliché. ("Fast and sweet" or "Give it to me—just once" at times replaced the more familiar phrase.)

These professional detectives knew what I was investigating and they knew the caseload they already had and what could be expected by day's end. They allotted proportional time as the seriousness of the case demanded, which in my case was minimal. I showed the detective what I had found and he pointed to the corner holding cell in the squad room where four men were being held on some charge or other. It seemed obvious who the perpetrator could be among those detained. He had on a long sleeved red sweater that had a yellow hue to it! I said to myself, *"Mister, your days are numbered; you are not going anywhere soon."* It had to be an open-and-shut case under the worst of circumstances—a shoo-in—to be sure!

If only these serendipitous happenings would occur in real cases, the more serious cases, this criminalistics field of endeavor could be fun, I mused.

I was to find out time and time again that these happy chance happenings, these desirable discoveries, these interlinked episodes did occur by accident with some frequency, but either few bothered to notice them or they did not know what, who, or how, when or where to capitalize on such discoveries. As I was to find out, in most instances it is always safest to go by the book, chapter and verse, but no book in existence had taken any notice serious enough to even mention this possibility except "the stories"—the folklore and the war stories some were willing to tell but only during the academic lectures.

For reasons of expediency, it would have been faster for the squad detective to turn the sweater the prisoner was wearing over to me for delivery to the crime lab, but I wanted no part in that "chain of evidence" and told the insistent, overworked detective as gently as I could, that in no way was I going to take possession of the sweater at this point in time. If we were to go to trial, I wanted no excuses to be given to any defense attorney that any cross-contamination had occurred (between the sweater and the closely held fibers I found) in the squad room or any time after the incident. It was critical to safeguard and avoid these possible contact points until the evidence was placed in more competent hands. With good investigative techniques, the only point of contamination was before the incident, as the accused carried the brick and threw it at the window that I had just examined. Little did I realize that the question of possible cross-contamination would never be in question; this case and many like it would never reach the courthouse.

Upon returning to the laboratory at the end of a busy day, the proper sequence was followed to process the various cases, special care being given to any case involving blood, firearms, and document evidence. These items were never dusted for latent fingerprints until the experts from these sections had at least inspected the evidence in question in order to avoid the loss of any latent evidence.[4] The fibers in the attempted burglary were turned over to the serology section in a secure and routine manner.

As time and interest permitted, a person could keep track of a handful of cases that he had been assigned to and remain knowledgeable as the case was processed from one expert to another as circumstances required. Since the attempted burglary case was to go to court for the initial hearing and setting of the trial date, I paid close attention to its progress. I was, after all, deliberately and unavoidably in the chain of evidence. Much to my surprise, only a shallow conclusion was reached in the laboratory analysis and written report; the sweater worn by the defendant contained "similar fibers" when compared to those found at the scene imbedded in the glass window. "In a city of 8 million people, there have to be hundreds of sweaters just like this one; no two dissimilar from this one," I was told when I questioned the terminology contained in the report. Satisfied that the correct decision had been made, I responded to the court subpoena for the preliminary hearing. The assigned detective knowingly read the experts' report and reported to the court that "the people" did not have sufficient evidence for the identification of the suspect to the burglary and all charges were dismissed. (The security guard was not absolutely sure of his identification.) In future years, I was to participate in and witness many similar situations and did nothing about them for a long time—too long.

It had been a minor case and only minor property damage resulted from the activities of this perpetrator. There were to be other more important cases with far more serious consequences, but the outcome in far too many of them was to be the same. The analysts in these cases were knowledgeable professionals who were doing their jobs and they needed the "accidentals"—the marks of specific identification—and these were not there and nothing more could be done about it. These cases were to be filed away and considered to be closed. The standards of objective judgment were to be kept very high.

The commonality in so many of these cases seemed to be that the individual has rights only after that person has been charged with a crime. The victims and their rights become less than periphereal to the entire process, incredibly isolated if not forgotten in the circumstances that most concern them.

MEANINGFUL DISCLOSURES

1. An acceptable definition of criminalistics would be that it is a discipline that uses and applies the principles of biology, chemistry, and physics to law and to law enforcement. (See Chapter Nine and its footnote #1.)

2. U.S. vs. Wilson (441 F. 2d 655, 1971) and this court decision supercedes any contrary decisions on the part of any crime laboratory director, police department administrative policies, or professional organizations, unless there is an arrogant (unlawful?) usurpation of administrative power just for power's

sake. For example, IAI—footnote #5 in paper as published in June 1982.

3. These crime scene field teams (forensic) are the eyes, ears, and feet of a crime laboratory and whose members are usually "generalists" in the criminalistic profession. These are individuals who have a broad knowledge of almost all crime laboratory work units and they apply this general knowledge at crime scenes when they select or otherwise identify important items of evidence for further laboratory examination. The more in-depth evidence examinations are then performed by "in house specialists" who have a much deeper understanding of one or more areas of concentration. These experts usually remain in the laboratory in order to maximize their time and talents. It is not at all unusual for a member of a field team to become an "in-house expert" in some laboratory specialty after gaining practical experience in the field.

4. In many such instances great harm can be done to items of evidence that are "improperly handled." For example, if a weapon is dusted for latent fingerprints before a firearms expert has examined it, the dusting powder could add unneeded confusion to the expert's opinion as to whether the gun has or has not been recently fired—evidenced from the presence of gunpowder in the barrel of the weapon. If the weapon was not dusted prior to his physical examination, any powder residue visible in the barrel would be gunpowder; if blood is thought to be present on a weapon, the gun should not be dusted for latent prints prior to its examination by a serologist since the powder could interfere with his chemical testing procedures. When these examinations are made, each specialist must complete his task without disturbing any latent prints that might be on the weapon. Likewise, evidence that is "fugitive" must also be given special handling to prevent it from vanishing; for example, evidence must be kept away from any heat, and blood evidence (blood samples and bloody clothing) needs to be refrigerated until the examiner has

24

time to start its analysis; moist clothing must be air dried in a secured, clean location prior to storage; extensive photographs taken of any item or situation that cannot be preserved or physically presented in court, such as crime scene photographs of all kinds, very large pieces of evidence such as bloody (plastic) prints on the wall of a subway car in which a homicide has occurred, et cetera.

Chapter 3

DEATH ON NEPTUNE AVENUE

If you limit your actions to things that no one can possibly find fault with, you will not do much.

—Lewis Carroll

A consideration of petty circumstances is the tomb of great things.

—Voltaire

In a large, distant city bustling with activity and night life, the last day of the week had arrived. With anticipation, the citizens approached the weekend with enthusiasm, anxious to spend a productive day that, hopefully, would mirror the approaching weekend.

As so many thousands of her citizens frustratingly passed these sunlight hours at their professional pursuits, the city breathed with activity and purpose. The hands of the clock could not be pushed but they did move forward at a snail's pace. Finally, the week was ended; "masks" worn for these hours in the work week could be set aside and the intervening trip home through the city traffic endured.

It was quitting time in the insurance business and its employees were beginning to make their homeward journey.

A young girl about twenty-four years old is easily distinguished in this homeward bound crowd that starts to fill the streets and the city's exit points. She is a blond, with long, almost straight hair held in place by a ribbon that seems to be out of place, matched against the red overcoat the girl was now wearing. The ribbon was precisely chosen in this morning's dressing routine to match the blue print dress and blue shoes the young accountant wore this business day. Once the coat was stored for the day, this pert college graduate mixed well in the business atmosphere of this busy concern. Her salary was better than average; not as high as she aspired to, but much better than most young women her age. The salary, however, didn't yet allow her the luxury to have matching street wear to the clothes she wore in the office.

She began her trip home and walked briskly with departing friends, each of them falling from her path as they turned in different directions for their evening activities. She, too, had a pleasant evening to look forward to and a long three-day weekend. The corner traffic light changed and she started to cross. A bus was coming from the opposite direction and she didn't want to miss it. She started to cross the wide avenue and had almost gained the opposite corner bus stop when a small white panel truck made a right turn on the green traffic signal. Had she departed her job a few seconds sooner or been delayed a few seconds more, had she combed her hair or sharpened a pencil or answered the phone one more time, her evening most probably would not have ended as it did.

As the small white panel truck turned the corner, it appeared that the driver must be totally blind. Did the brakes of the truck fail? Was he in that much of a hurry that he didn't see this human being? We will never know what brought these independents to cross paths, but the fatal accident evidently happened faster than it takes to describe it. The accident happened so quickly, it was a fact before anyone could draw a breath! The pretty young woman who had such a neat appearance and a personality to match was seen sprawled on Neptune Avenue, awkwardly laying on her red coat, her eyes closed and a small red stream of blood appearing at the corners of her mouth and ears. The red liquid gave evidence of the blow she just received and of the life she was now losing. The white panel truck somehow caught this person under its left front wheel and just stood there, seemingly waiting for some unseen but understanding device to lift it off, but nothing did lift the offending wheel off this human being. According to witnesses who were a moment before anticipating the arrival of a metro bus, the driver of the panel truck got out of the cab and noticed the woman under his front wheel. He immediately returned to the driver's seat and sped off in his intended direction. Most probably unknown to this heartless driver, he began to drag the girl's body, for it had somehow become locked with the wheel as he left the scene. When the scene was later examined, fragments, some not larger than specks of red cloth, were seen imbedded in the roadway. The sprinkled red fragments, evidently from the coat the girl was wearing, were found for some thirty feet. The gruesome scene so disturbed these eyewitness commuters, and the sequence of events happened so quickly no one was able to offer the responding police a car license number. The arriving bus shielded the girl's body from further damage by unsuspecting traffic and she laid there, midblock, until the arriving police placed a body bag over her lifeless body.

The first police car on the scene called in to the police radio dispatcher a description of the vehicle and direction of travel, but in the evening traffic it had vanished from sight. For several days the local press cooperated with the police in requesting public assistance to identify this white truck, but the descriptions available from the startled witnesses could have matched numerous people and vehicles. During the next two weeks, no fewer than eight white panel trucks were brought to the crime laboratory garage for processing. No evidence was found in any of them; the trucks were reassembled and released.

At the end of this time period, a police dispatcher received a call from a concerned citizen in response to the public notice that a white panel truck was wanted in the hit and run death of this now almost forgotten citizen. The caller inquired as to whether the police were still interested in the wanted notice she had heard on the radio a few days before. When the dispatcher said, "Yes, the police still want all the information they can get," the caller excitedly whispered that a white van, then well within her view, was making circular turns, almost as if deliberately going through mud puddles, in a large open area immediately in front and across the street from her home. Was the caller's attention drawn to this view because of the radio notice or to the somewhat peculiar aspect of a seeing a white truck become soiled in mud for no apparent purpose? A local police patrol car (RMP) was redirected from its normal patrol route to the address indicated by the concerned citizen and yet another driver and white panel truck worked its way into the police garage. The driver was to be identified and to be questioned by the police and the truck to be examined by laboratory personnel.

Initial examination of the vehicle revealed no physical damage to the front portion of the van. The left front tire was removed as was done so many times before on those other trucks. Nothing unusual was found. As was done in all the other cases, the other three wheels of this small vehicle were removed and processed. In the right rear wheel brake area was found what proved to be long strands of human blond hair and one small patch of red cloth material. The human hair could not be sexed nor could the laboratory experts make a "piece match" of the red cloth to any part of the red coat held in evidence due to the street damage to the coat and the small piece of evidence they had to work with. The subsequent written laboratory report submitted to the prosecutor's office stated that "Sufficiently individualizing characteristics were not present in the items submitted to make any positive identification in this case." The known and the unknown pieces in the case could not be technically brought together. Only a brief and passing notice was given to the observation that the pattern on the left front tire did not match the pattern on the other three wheels whose patterns were identical to each other as was the tire pattern on the spare tire found in the trunk of the vehicle. There was no thought given to the possibility of an obvious tire change having occurred after the front left wheel area had been cleaned of any debris. The driver and the truck were released and any thoughts of a prosecution were dismissed for lack of evidence and the case remains an open homicide case to this day.

The technical considerations given to this event were an overly benign interpretation of the known facts in the case. Such compulsive adherence to procedure relieved the analyst of responsibility for dealing with the real problem. The victims in this case and in so many similar cases deserve more than a perfunctory defense from the prosecution's expert witness. Modern technology must not deny its responsibilities to reality.

This author believes and would estimate that the chances of these items found on the right rear wheel area of this small white panel truck to be an unrelated mischance to the hit and run death on Neptune Avenue is in excess of one million to one against such circumstances accidentally duplicating themselves. It is far beyond any reasonable expectation that it could be otherwise. A very high correlation is all too apparent in these circumstances regardless of the technical imperfections. Lacking the needed accidental marks of individualization required for specific identification, these items were treated as if they were pieces of idle information rather than firm evidence of wrongdoing on the part of the delinquent driver. No insightful link between the truck innocently traveling through the mud puddles on a clear day and any prior felonious knowledge on the part of the driver was ever attempted by anyone. Since the case was not going to be submitted to a court of law due to these technical difficulties, the subjective observations screaming to be heard in defense of the innocent female victim were effectively silenced. To avoid these inductive observations and connections is a violation of any measure of reason, common sense, reality, or innate sense of justice to the victim. For these experts for the prosecution, upon literally stumbling over such salient evidence, not to attempt to bring this reality to the forefront and attempt to deal with it constructively is all but unforgiveable, wall to wall safety, except that there is no established system or other structure of choice to deal with such chance discoveries. This was to happen many times, in many different circumstances where the victims did not receive the benefit of this silent evidence. These pressures for objective, error-free identification are as real as they are crippling to the luckless victims of circumstances. The fact that there always has been an unconscious lack of sympathy for a moral focus in these cases is more than obvious to anyone who considers this an important ingredient. The Law does not demand such and therefore it does not enter into any of the considerations given to these cases.

Some days later, information was received that the driver-owner of this truck had a record of a previous fatal hit-and-run accident. It was too gruesome to imagine; this latest case was bad enough.

Occasions like this made it seem as if we were somehow walking in a darkened maze at midday. Somehow we must not continue to be slaves to these circumstances that appear so regularly, but become their master. The feeling of frustration in cases such as this is extreme. This discontent is in reality a search for truth, but so far an unrewarding search and this concern for an ethical resolution to this conflict was to grow only with time, experience and thought.

As time passed it became apparent that a pattern of passivity had quietly developed in the criminalistics profession that was not pretty to look at; a vicious circle has engulfed us and there seem to be no other alternatives unless we rethink our foundations.

• If the profession of criminalistics is on firm ground, incriminating evidence can be found at most crime scenes. In most cases, some kind of evidence is found at these scenes, incomplete as it may appear to be.

• In reality, all too often the evidence found in a factual crime situation is less than complete. In most cases it lacks sufficient and specific identification marks or features that conclusively identify the perpetrator to the crime. In the real world, such crime scene situations are very untidy places in a very untidy world.

• Very few significant case decisions are made by laboratory personnel based on the harsh reality of the evidential traces received from these scenes. The evidence received in these cases in most instances is small, always contaminated and irreplaceable and is less than complete. Since these professional experts do require high levels of credibility—high "bench marks" in their decision-making processes and since they have been given no flexibilities or encouragement to deal with any contingencies or imperfections in the evidence, the majority of such imperfect cases are given minimum consideration. These impotent reporting methods do prevent the local criminal prosecutor from submitting such cases to a criminal court for jury review. When questioned as to the appropriateness of this situation, the normal response is that these analysts "want to be sure that only the correct individual is identified to the crime investigated." They strongly believe, as did the jurist William Blackstone, that "it is far better to release nine guilty persons than convict one innocent person." This is thought to be a morally asymmetrical bankrupt concept of the self-deluded because there is no regard for or notice taken as to what these nine were guilty of!

If we as a society are so concerned not to injure one innocent person, why do we not lower the traffic speed limit from fifty-five miles per hour to thirty-five and materially reduce the predictable and staggering numbers of tragic auto deaths and serious long-term personal injuries that do occur each year, especially to the young?

Then as now we have to maintain a certain placid indifference for these serious auto victims if present-day society is to survive at "acceptable levels." Likewise, every airline passenger constantly accepts a daily calculated, personal risk of becoming a crash victim in their selected mode of convenient air travel. No one questions that there are constant risks in normal life situations but, rather, at what level are these risks acceptable? In all of our normal circumstances there is an acceptance of calculated risks in our lives. Can we criminalists, in good conscience—in an adversarial system of justice—dare treat the victims of criminal violence with the same cavalier attitude and allow the prosecutor or the jury in a court of law to decide the level of acceptable risk? In order to bring justice to the victims it would seem to be mandatory to do so.

• The less than certain cases do not go to court because little or no notice is taken of the silent, tacit, strategic connections present in such evidence. If viewed with a discerning eye, much of the evidence contains information of high inherent integrity and compatibility that can be available if the material reality in the evidence is viewed with inductive, intuitive reasoning processes, in addition to the all-present objective, deductive processes now so current and professionally existing in laboratory analyses. At the present time, however, there is now no existing decision matrix for the experts to deal with this compatible fragmented evidence that is less than complete or scientifically perfect. There is also no desire by these prosecution experts to confront the opposition without having faultless evidence since few wish to withstand the flak in defending an imperfect case from any energetic defense attorney regardless of the reason; therefore, the system remains the ineffective failed monopoly that it always has been. No inductive, subjective reasoning schemes or projections are used and correspondingly no use of embodied experiences, or use of any personal probability reflecting this experience, is even considered by anyone. This is rational, methodical, inert thinking that neglects any personal or moral responsibility to the victims of criminal violence and renders any boldness in criminal court testimony all but impossible and this is thought to be a national disgrace. There is never any attempt to consider the possible existence of any hidden agendas that might exist in any of these cases. This certainly must be considered a poor investigative technique. Without a doubt the present criminal justice system is not a victim driven organization!

• The criminal trial juries are prevented from viewing the incomplete evidence because little value is placed on it and it is not submitted to the county prosecutor or to a grand jury, or if submitted, it is not in the form in which it could be used in a court of law and not even a hint is given that many times such presentations could be different. When this happens there most definitely is an abuse of the rule of law since any court review process has been unilaterally expunged from the proceedings. All such cases are now written off as "insufficient evidence for complete analysis;" "No conclusion can be made due to the insufficiency of the evidence." The cases are, in essence, closed by the laboratory—in the laboratory—and the trial juries are not able to voice the communities' conscience on such matters. Their options to do so have been preempted—in the crime laboratory—by this unlimited usurpation of their power. These rigid, distorted decisions are being made and the difficult compelling presentations are being avoided in court for the comfort of the expert, not that of the victim who has appealed to the state for help and for retribution. The all-consuming quest for certainty is a major obstacle to solving the problems that arise in most criminal cases. To allow these experts to exercise this power defeats the very foundation of the jury system. If we remember Clemenceau's timely aphorism addressing a duplicate situation that "war is too important to be left to the generals," then by extension we can safely say that "final decisions as to fact in any criminal case are (also) too important to be left to any of these experts." If this is not a totally true observation, then society would not need our present-day trial jury system and would only need a judge to hear the evidence in the case from witnesses and these experts and he would make the judgments as to the facts in the case and render an appropriate sentence according to law. Obviously, society has made the firm and lasting judgment that not even the judge is qualified to render that service!

• The victims in the cases not addressed are left unattended because they have no appeal from these actions, since there are no legal or case review processes of these negative case decisions. The victim's rights in our advocatory system of law become secondary to the traditional needs of the analyst and these self-absorbed, narrowly focused analysts have become experts by default. They take no risks; they initiate nothing and accept little personal (or moral) responsibility for the outcome of the cases they are being paid to examine. This private reality collides with and is totally irreconcilable with the public's image of professional scientific detection. If there are technical voids in the evidence, professional chemists are not permitted to make reference to previous case learning experiences, couplings, linkages, or adduce critical recognition of severed relationships that might be present in the material evidence. Total objectivity with no back-filling of the natural voids using a legitimate leap in logic (an interrelated gestalt closure) is permitted or thought to be possible at any time or under any circumstances. As experts for the prosecution, our professional lives should be intrinsically linked to the victims of criminal violence. This relationship is a challenge requiring our clear understanding and strong commitment to them. This new sphere of understanding demands that we not censor the truth that does exist in the imperfect evidence and recognize that the missing perspective is that the victims have civil rights too and are equal citizens of this republic. There seems to be a gross misunderstanding in these laboratories by these professional chemists (with their fixed and immutable ideas) of their roles in this advocatory system of justice and their implicit obligations to the victims of criminal violence.[1] When nine guilty people are released, the needs of the nine victims[2] in the associated cases are completely ignored and this is viewed as a denial of basic due process of law for these victims because they have equal needs and rights for protection under law. These victims of criminal violence are being discounted as a valued consideration in our present system of criminal justice. The nine guilty defendants are being sheltered (released) from justice by our humanitarianism and its perverted sense of justice to the victims. In reality the system is doing far more to protect the guilty parties from retribution than it is protecting the "innocent" from unjust confinement. There is no understanding of either the moral ramifications or the legal consequences of this victim neglect.

• Additional crimes are then committed by the released suspects and the system inadvertently makes it possible for more victims to be created. All members of society depend on the law to solve these arrest problems and the foregoing is a miserable example of abandoning the innocent majority and is such a ludicrous situation as to be incapable of rebuttal. A vicious circle of re-victimization has been constructed and few in our timorous bureaucracies care to notice it. The prosecutor as the advocate for the victim[3] is helpless unless he is given the necessary evidence in proper form from either the police or the crime laboratory. All too often the words of long ago ring true in these instances;

For the want of a nail, the shoe was lost;
For the want of a shoe, the horse was lost;
For the want of a horse, the battle was lost.

In the vast majority of criminal cases, a comprehensive proactive crime laboratory report is "the nail" the prosecutor must have to initiate legal proceedings against any suspect. In the absence of such reports it is too easy to see that these victims are being violated twice. Once when they accidentally become victims of criminal violence and a second time when they or their close relatives appeal for assistance to the established criminal justice system and they are denied this needed assistance by the very system that is supposed to help them. These public servants have a high regard for their own longevity and a higher mental attitude to avoid all risks and this is accomplished by issuing these timid reports when it most often could be otherwise. A great miscarriage of justice is being perpetrated on these victims when imperfect evidence, justified by contemporary experience, is not used in a court of law to help convict the suspects. The incomplete evidence is treated as if it were inoperative knowledge, which is not the case; rather, it is that we are operating in a technical vacuum and not dealing with normal case complications and with the associated *real life* situations. To avoid these decisions is not harmless error but a safety strategy that reflects small amounts of independence and courage and lots of automatic conformity by these criminal court experts. In the process of doing so, justice is being kidnapped.

There seems to be a piercing need to review the fundamentals of the profession because the victims of criminal violence are not being given their day in court when imperfect circumstantial evidence is ignored. This is a violation of the victim's fundamental right to have such a hearing before a jury of their peers when they are feloniously injured. A serious contributing factor seems to be a sniff of a professional elitism in existing current examinations, an excuse for extreme exactness that is suitable for pure science but is too limiting for such an applied science as criminalistics. Some other set of variables that recognizes as credible the co-existence of less than complete evidence and which will work more effectively with science to find the desired, the needed truth, must be developed within the framework of the profession. For the victim's sake we must not allow reality to be blurred or allow ourselves to be ineffective tools of fate. We have not been grappling with the harsh reality so obviously present in these cases. As stewards for society we are indifferent to the struggle; professionally we are above it! For some reason, we have not been bold enough, realistic enough, or imaginative enough to examine in detail the pressures on the state expert's decision-making process or the structure and process in which these decisions are made. To date, these areas have been inaccessible and are areas with which few supervisors or crime laboratory managers argue or wrestle. We speak here of the vacillation in the decision-making process required of these experts, especially in difficult, imperfect cases that cannot reach practical certainty and beyond. For any court expert to issue a report *only* on that which is obviously certain or "beyond a scientific doubt," objective certitude is merely dutiful loyalty to the system and is completely self-serving and is the path of least resistance. Such experts are caught up in the fascination of analyzing completed patterns (cases), without ever giving dialogue or expressing one's belief in degrees of inductive, internalized probability to the less than perfect (patterns) cases. Basically, the profession has not resisted the dangers of concrete thinking and rigid conformity because thinking in black and white (extremes) is easier than in shades of gray. There has been a replacement of intelligent, subjective thought[4] by routine and we have become experts only in the noncontroversial cases because of our subjective indifference to the needs of the victims of violent crimes. The search for ethical truth in such cases was totally neglected.[5]

We need to bridge the gap between what is reasonable probability and that which is scientific certainty, addressing each case in calibrated increments and render to the courts and juries the advisory opinions (informed judgments) required, based on the evidence and our abilities (accumulated experience) to relate to its realities. We must have the courage and intiative to leave the safe, scientific nursery (an atmosphere free from all errors, addressing nothing that is not absolutely or obviously certain, abstract, and intelligently satisfying) and render to the criminal justice system more substantive communications giving objectively reasonable risk assessment to the majority of imperfect criminal cases within our jurisdictions. Since very few experts or crime laboratories follow this theme (see Chapter 12—the oe factor), it is absolutely critical to correct these basic, long standing and dangerous weaknesses in our present system of justice.

Rather than be driven by purely legal consideration, the criminal court experts are being fallaciously guided by administrative dictates, contrary to the interests of the victims (powerless/voiceless) and of the courts, such timid policies having no basis (finding) in law since it is just more convenient to all concerned simply to ignore the less than perfect cases. As criminal court experts, these platonic guardians of justice strive for overwhelming proofs using only deductive reasoning, allowing no inductive interpretation or extrapolation of their past casework experiences or learned insights to be present in their thinking process or in their reports. The technical reports emanating from many crime laboratories are superficial, noncontroversial, safe, decision-making documents with little or no deep convictions expressed. Such reporting suppresses the reliable and probative evidence that is available. Such experts rarely place their reputations at hazard in an effort to serve justice, the victims or the courts. There is no vicarious suffering with the victims in these instances.

As seen in chart 2, only those criminal cases retroactively capable of reaching scientific certainty, "J," ever reach the criminal courts for jury consideration! The vast majority of cases, "C-H," failing to reach objective certainty, are always turned back and *eliminated* from any legal review, thus avoiding most tensions in future court appearances. These are cases to which adequate crime laboratory response has not been made. Society and the victims are the worse for this act of omission due to a lack of courage and faith in our system of law. The analyst has avoided all risks, accepted no responsibilities, and has exhibited

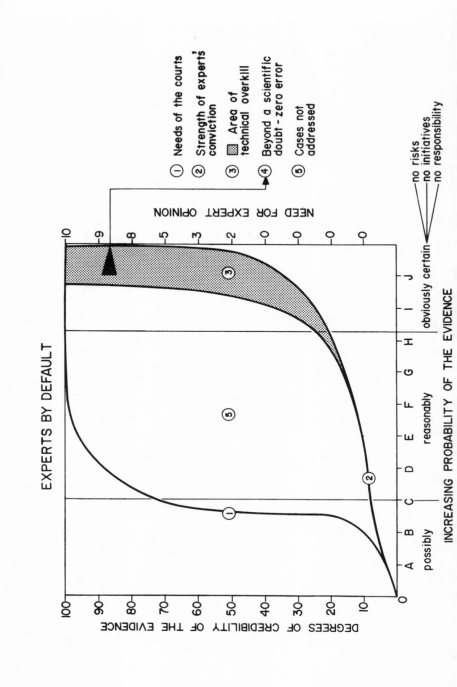

EXPERTS BY DEFAULT

NEED FOR EXPERT OPINION

① Needs of the courts
② Strength of experts' conviction
▓ Area of technical overkill
④ Beyond a scientific doubt - zero error
⑤ Cases not addressed

no risks
no initiatives
no responsibility

DEGREES OF CREDIBILITY OF THE EVIDENCE

INCREASING PROBABILITY OF THE EVIDENCE

possibly   reasonably   obviously certain

little initiative. A safe decision has been made. No disablement of chemical theory is permitted but exaggerations, for the safety of the expert, abound.

The crux of the controversy is the acceptance of positions of absolutism, "zero error," and "beyond a scientific doubt," and associated negativisms. Such actions strongly imply that there can be only one unquestionable position which rejects any thought that a criminal trial is an arena of disputes and contentions in which any hidden agendas are to be exposed. It is idealism—mistaken and misplaced; it is secular humanism at its very worst. The tragic truth is that we do not have to remain in these positions since they are sure to fail proposals and we do have the means for it to be otherwise.

MEANINGFUL DISCLOSURES

1. In the present Criminal Justice System there are few advocates for the victims of criminal violence. The education of a professional chemist does not encompass or stress an understanding that the superordinate goal of the advocatory system is justice for all parties. The advocatory system is not a debating society nor a system for conflict resolutions, compromise or arbitration as in a labor dispute or family quarrel. The system must have knowledgeable professionals who are "not afraid to get their hands dirty" for society's benefit, under law. See Chapter Nine and its footnote #3.

2. These needs are for justice, retribution, vindication, and peace of mind in the particular incident and for the future. In reality, however, the present system of justice does more to protect the guilty from retribution than protect the innocent from unjust confinement since the present system is so easily circumscribed with almost no resistance from the prosecution. Examples of this

institutionalized abdication of responsibilities abound in this text.

3. Very few prosecutors in the criminal justice system view themselves as advocates for the victims of criminal violence. For the most part they are as passive and as self protecting of their reputations as any prosecution expert mentioned in these pages; there is very little shared responsibility with the victims in their hour of need.

4. Intelligent "subjectivity" accepts the principle that we do need our scientific anchors and roots but it also does not discount experience, inductive thinking, and professional common sense in the learning process. See Chapter Six and its footnote #4 and Chapter Seven and its footnote #4.

5. The strands of human blond hair and the red cloth had intimate interconnectiveness (to this hit and run death) that irritated few consciences because the "technical necessities" were not there. It is common in such analyses that no attempt is made to "see" the "at-oneness" connection in this evidence which would produce a strong link between the vehicle and the victim. The physical search of all the panel trucks was useless and a waste of time since nothing was really accomplished with any evidential material when it was found. Such ineffective crime laboratories are indeed very expensive collection and storage facilities. Any reasonable expectations that might arise were pre-doomed by an inability, an unwillingness to act, and "see" the comprehensive aspects in the evidence.

Chapter 4

THE BACKGROUND SETTING

An observer who is a realist has a two-fold task. He must report what he observes and he must make sure that his report is relevant, that is, that it concerns the particular entity, state of affairs, processes that he happens to be interested in. The first demand requires him to keep as closely as possible to "what he sees." The second demand requires him to interpret his report as concerning an objective state affairs, i.e., to say more than just what he sees.
—R. Colony

The car is rolling along nicely on this clear summer night, but I can see a weather change coming in the distant hills, many lightning streaks crossing the broad desert sky. *We must be going to have a storm before I reach home tonight,* I think to myself and take in the view of the vast distance ahead. Indian Junction is coming into view and it is an early stop for supper when going north. It is the only stop, in either direction, for the next 120 miles, so as usual I take advantage of an early meal. Had I been going south from Flagstaff, it would be a more welcome sight indicating that my lonesome trip would be almost at an end. As it is, going north, my trip to the hills and home has barely begun.

After getting a light meal, I guide the car back onto the highway and my system is prepared now for the two-and-a-half hour ride still ahead. I become mesmerized again by the silence and the hum of the night wind against a slightly opened window and the now automatic motions of hand and foot allow me to return deep in thought.

As the state's expert witness in criminal cases, a criminalist is supposed to give support to both the police and the prosecutor's office as the technical advisor on the circumstantial evidence found at most crime scenes. The actual education and training of a new criminalist begins by requiring that each one have a technical background so that at least the fundamentals for future learning are in place. At the crime laboratory, as the in-house, on-the-job training takes place, three main premises suggested by early pioneers in the field are demonstrated.

An early pioneer, a well-known French "criminalist," A. Bertillon by name, was an expert in identification as it was then practiced at the turn of the century. He had expertise in document examinations as well as other technical endeavors.[1] Due to his early position and formidable efforts, many questions arose to which answers had to be formulated in order for the young professional to advance. One such perplexing and recurring problem was to determine when an examiner could, with some strength of conviction, consider an identification certain. The considerations Bertillon was to give were to have a strong, almost lasting influence on establishing the lower limits permitted for certain identification. The ever perfect number "12"[2] became the significant bench mark establishing indisputable certainty. Bertillon had the full range of numbers to pick from and he chose "12" as being a better minimum limit than "11," but it could with equal ease have been "15"! It was just a number (a meaningful number) but it was to become, as it were, the Maginot Line, above which was certainty and therefore analytical safety and below which could be disaster or calamity; certainly some risk to those who would dare to challenge this advice. For the many who did not stay current with subsequent studies and for those outside the discipline, "the twelve-point rule" became the significant rule of thumb for almost all types of forensic identification purposes especially in the then new art of fingerprint identification.[3] As the years passed, this "magic number" became for a lazy analyst the minimum level for identification in any worthwhile analysis.

Not realizing that further development in the art of fingerprint identification would consider not only the twelve points but other rare patterns and other newly developed combinations to be far more significant identification, the strict twelve point rule slowly became outdated as an historical accident that lasted too long. Experts in future criminal fingerprint identification cases, depending on which of these many variables were present in their latent identifications, were to present their opinion evidence in a court of criminal law using seven or eight points. Eventually, it was to be acknowledged that there was no specific level above or below which certainty could be reached. It all depended on the circumstances and the strength of the expert's professional opinion. Any defense attorney who would disagree with this determination, of course, could present his own opposing expert fingerprint examiner to counter the state's contention of identification. However, the misinterpretation of this rule remained prominent in many people's minds. Bertillon's reasoning that twelve points were better than eleven for identification had merit but for the uninformed, the fainthearted, or those working outside the field; it became the standard, below which very few identifications were attempted or even considered. In reality, we have not reached certainty with the twelve-to-fifteen points anymore than we have missed certainty if we have ten or eleven points if a trial jury believes the prosecution's expert.

The trigger point of decision is relative both to the examiner and any member of the jury. The criminal courts do not require that certainty be reached before a jury hears the opinion of the expert. If the bench mark for decision making in such matters is too high, the case will never see the inside of a court room, where the real decisions should be made. The item not considered by most uncritical analysts is that any given case is to be decided by a jury; the total composite of all the pertinent evidence convincing each individual juror that the sum total exceeds his individual and their collective threshold of believability, which establishes for them a level of belief that is "beyond a reasonable doubt." Any given, individual piece of evidence presented to the jury is but a contribution to that final sum or jury judgment. It is to be a jury decision—not a decision to be made, established, or withheld by any analyst secure in any crime laboratory.

A second, likewise famous French pioneer in early "criminalistics" was an individual named Locard, a notable peer of Bertillon. He postulated that "every perpetrator of a crime leaves something of himself at every crime scene and/or takes something away with him from every crime scene." If this is a correct observation in almost each and every instance, if either or both of these items are found, it will help identify the associated individual as the perpetrator of the specific crime. The bottom line to this idea is to simply "look" for any item at a crime scene that is there and should not be there, and/or look for any item that is not there but that should be there and take advantage of these opportunities when and where presented. Locard postulated that there are tensions perpetually existing between the perpetrator of a crime, the actual crime (scene), and the technical crime (scene) investigator, and that the culprit will most often fail in his attempt to conceal his personal participation in the crime. It is left for the investigator to discover these uncontrollable, broken artifacts inadvertently left at the scene if he is to meet his responsibilities to society. It is a recognition that there is an intrinsic interdependence between any perpetrator and the items of evidence left at or taken from the crime scene and that the verification of such can be well within our locus of control. This can be seen as looking for the hidden agenda. Everything is based on the assumption of being rational, logical, and reasonable and that with prudent extrapolations to such conclusions, the analyst does not need to be perfect in all respects of that determination. This would be a gestalt closure when an investigator comprehensively reviews a crime (scene) and is able to solve the puzzle (to his own and to a jury's satisfaction) without having all the pieces to the puzzle he would like to have; that is, being able to "read the scene" in spite of the natural voids or contrived circumstances that to others are irreconcilable voids which for them renders "the evidence" useless.[4]

A quick example of the above attitude would be a criminal investigation of a suspected arson case. All too often, a fire is used to conceal a more basic crime with the intention that any evidence left at the original crime scene would be destroyed in a fire and if executed properly, no evidence of an arson would be noticeable. Upon examination of an otherwise "innocent" fire, Locard's principle comes into its own. A legitimate arson fire is set to destroy the valuable property of another. Upon investigation of the scene, a concerned forensic investigator is interested if there are in the remains of the fire expensive machinery, paintings, jewelry, cash in the register, and the contents of a fireproof safe secure. Such items, although badly damaged, should not be missing from their natural locations! Are regular business records at least recognizable? Have the utilities and their potential energies been misdirected to cause or support the fire? Are the victims, if any, in appropriate locations in the building, not locked together in some room? Finding or not finding such items at the scenes in their proper places is absolutely critical. Any apparent disorder or irregularities become meaningfully obvious as self-evident events of some other, additional unlawful activities (a burglary-arson or a grand larceny by the owners for insurance purposes) if sympathetic creativity, instead of benevolent neutrality, is encouraged, taught, rewarded, desired, pursued, and demanded. No written policy could possibly cover the unlimited evidential possibilities available in this case and for the correct situation if one is not open to other than prescribed dogma.

With the wind blowing, the cooler night air comes into the car as it starts the climb up these hills to "God's country" and the driver continues to ponder the early development of his profession. His mind recalls the tale of a famous bacteriologist by the name of A. Fleming who, in 1929, had a lasting effect on his own profession. This researcher accidentally discovered penicillin and opened to a hungry world the potent field of mycology and the associated antibiotics that were to be developed from the study of various molds and fungi.

Fleming and his co-workers had been studying the life cycles of various strains of bacteria. For some unknown reason, a lapse in routine occurred and a culture in a glass dish was accidentally left uncovered. A desirable but serendipitous event happened! An unexpected, "unwanted" contamination took place that under any other circumstance would have been a disaster. An unknown mold had accidentally blown in and taken root in the culture dish and killed the bacteria under study. Fleming, upon seeing the "zone of inhibition"[5] questioned the unusual observation and investigated the incident in detail. He took advantage of "opportunities" as they presented themselves regardless of the direction from which they came. When asked years later, as he basked in the light of notoriety, how did he know what he had found when he found it? How did this fantastic discovery happen? Mr. Fleming simply stated that: "Chance comes only to the prepared mind."[6]

He freely admitted that his education, training, and obvious dedication had, in themselves, little to do with the actual discovery; chance had to play its role and that the chance happening had to be recognized and acted upon when the opportunity presented itself with a living belief that the course of nature has a fixed order in which nothing interferes with its ultimate continuation. He, like any other observer of the scene, had to be thoroughly familiar with the normal in order to interpret the unusual, the abnormal, or the inappropriate and then to extrapolate into the new. He had confidence that nature's behavior was so consistent that he could make plausible assumptions into the unknown that would have significant probabilities of succeeding. We will never know if some similar dedicated professional had the same experience fifteen years earlier but failed to see the opportunity and missed the move.

What was it that Fleming had that others didn't possess? The explanation was to become so obvious to others of his peers after he had shown the way! He had a trained mind, open to accept new information and interpret the unusual, the abnormal, the chance happenings with confidence in the order, the high predictability and continuity in nature, which from his previous exposures and experiences were well established and confirmed. He had to be thoroughly familiar with the normal in order to interpret the unusual or the abnormal and then to extrapolate into the new unknown area. These lucky mishaps were but insights to a smooth, natural, interdependent system that can be deciphered with close observations, patience, effort, and integrity. He knew when he observed his destroyed culture that there had to be a reasonable, compatible, rational answer to his keen yet un-answered observations.

The mishap was an unanticipated opportunity to spy deeper into nature's unyielding laws and systems. Archimedes did; Kepler did; Fermi did; Einstein did; Goddard did; Bessel did; Adams did and LeVerrici (Neptune) did; G. Pizzi did; Halley did; Landsteiner did; Marconi did; and Roentgen did, too. They used inductive, interpretive imagining of the mind (relevant imagery), rational reasoning to seek the truth by challenging the constructs of their minds with the reality, the serendipitous situations they were exposed to. They each revealed that what we learn from each experience depends to a large extent on the philosophy that each brings to that experience.

Due to his (Fleming's) philosophy, knowledge, and experi-ences, he was not uncomfortable or so insecure as not to follow a new, untraveled road. They each had witnessed a random event within a predictable reciprocal matrix that permitted a convergence of their past experiences, common sense, and reality to form a continuity of relationships; they (he) had confidence that "it" was but a link in a yet unexplored chain that had accidentally been exposed to their view; they acknowledged that we cannot unknow a known and that each of us must at least try to know an unknown, if it follows logical, anticipatory patterns yet unknown to us. The strongest motivation to follow this uncharted branch was the self confidence in the strong predictability inherent in the internal dynamics of the system they were familiar with and they then made the needed creative logical leap. Fleming knew as did they, that the heretofore processes of interdependent functions, truly concentrated and interwoven in mutual support, reflected a coordinating clockwork in the universe. Fleming recognized that all actions do have collateral or lineal consequences and that there was much more to nature than just physiochemical events. They accepted the situation and looked for the unusual, the invisible, the uncontrollable item in the mosaic and having an open psychic attitude dealt with the situation as an authentic carrier of reality. The continuous union and its dependent pieces, due to uncontrolled circumstances are, overwhelmingly probable, a disrupted pattern of the mosaic when found broken apart.

Converting Fleming's fortunate experience to criminalistics, the expert must seize the opportunity with confidence when it presents itself in at least an inquisitive, if not a knowledgeable manner. They must correlate their internal endogenous data base by sifting their personal experiences, grasp that the precursors that are so often present in these criminal cases do have a high correlation coefficient and then be assertive in their presentations. Without this recognition of the opportunity, without the acceptance of the personal responsibility to act when circumstances warrant it, the serendipitous accidents, the hidden agendas will become lost to us and to the victims of criminal violence. The resulting perversion of justice will continue if these professionals abdicate their responsibilities to reveal the truth.

Another characteristic that a criminalist must accept is to have compassion for the misery that daily confronts him and take advantage of the opportunistic circumstances that surround him. Compassion and empathy for the victims with the realization that the state, as represented by him, will never have all the pieces to any puzzle nor all the witnesses we need or would like to have to solve any given case. The authentic criminalist, being aware of this uncomfortable truth, has an inescapable burden to extend himself because it is he who has "to go in harm's way" to present to a jury a case with less than total certainty. It is he who is the court expert and in order to function properly he must be proactive and give his morally sincere opinion to the best of his ability. To avoid or ignore these circumstances will severely diminish the effectiveness of the prosecutors case and we all will miss the treasures inherent in this profession.

As experts, we must understand that Bertillon's "twelve-point rule" is just a number, a perfect number, better than none, one of many, fewer than most—but only a goal, not a destination. From Fleming we know we must anxiously await, with an alert apprehensiveness, the unexpected—"the happy accident"—and with compassion for the victims and for this silent evidence give an audible report to the needs of these victims in a court of criminal law. In doing so, the fifty to one ratio (50:1) of police case reports to convictions will be responsibly lowered to a level that justice demands. We must not retain shortsightedness that denies the behavioral interrelationships that do exist synergistically in nature and consequently in the evidence received at any crime laboratory.

The criminal courts recognize that there are many areas of human endeavor that are beyond the normal knowledge and experience of an empaneled jury and, therefore, there is a need for expert testimony to explain the evidence found at any crime scene. This circumstantial evidence is needed because eyewitness testimony, although thought to be essential, is often unreliable, especially at times of severe stress; confessions obtained from defendant(s) prior to trial can be recanted or minimized by the defense to the jury. The courts also recognize that certainty is an unrealistic ideal and that if a very high bench mark-trigger point is required, we as a society would make few, if any, decisions.

Overwhelming reality requires both the services of an expert to interpret and present the facts and those of a jury to make the final decision as to the truth of these facts. As the prosecutor's (state) expert, criminalists are as much a part of the complaint process as are the police and the victims themselves.

MEANINGFUL DISCLOSURES

1. As an early "scientific" investigator, Bertillon attempted to apply objective differentiable criteria to identify prisoners based on several physical measurements. His system was superceded in 1903 when Will West and William West, two federal prisoners in the same institution, were found to have the same measurements. As an early pioneer, Bertillon was involved in the celebrated Dreyfus case in France in 1899 with Emile Zola and his *J'Accuse* episode.

2. In the academic English literature that most college students are required to read, the numbers 3, 7, and 11 are so recurrent that they have long ago been considered to be "magic numbers." Likewise, for unknown reasons the number 12 has many advocates. The 12 categories in the Zodiac; the 12 labors of Hercules; 12 gods of Olympus; the 12 tribes of Israel; the 12 Apostles; the 12 days of Christmas; 12 items in a dozen; 12 months in a year; 12 baskets were left in Matt. 14–18; there are 12 inches to a foot of measurement; 12 moons of Jupiter; 12 pieces in the game of chess; 12 items on a clock.

3. Accepting this rule gave practitioners a formalism that was beautifully arrogant and reconfirmed that only that which was physically measurable existed (empiricism). Accepting this formula for immutable identification forever corrupted the new profession with its lamentable consequences that will be illustrated in these pages. It is a self-induced dysfunctional situation.

4. This would be very similar to the functioning of the synapse in our human nervous system. In the anatomy of our automatic nervous system there are minute spaces between the terminal ends of nerve fibers. The "empty" space between the end (axon) of a neuron and the beginning of a dendrite has no ability to communicate a nerve message to the dendrite until the nerve impulse in the neuron builds to a pressure so intense that it overcomes the resistance of the "empty" space and jumps and passes over the "void" or synapse—without the two nerve endings ever meeting or touching. The wider the synapse the more pressure build-up is necessary before a jump can be made.

In theory, this similar action takes place when the forensic examiner, using his normal tools of inspection, collection, and analyses comes to a reasonable opinion by synthesizing the information in the case. The internal congruence of the separated parts or the totality of the missing parts is so heavy and obvious to him, that the void that often does exist can be filled and conclusions made and his opinion given to a jury for their collective judgments. (See Chapter Eight and its footnote #2 and Chapter Nine and its footnote #1 as examples of the decision process, and Chapter Twelve and its footnote #1 for Richter Scale comparisons.)

5. This is an area in the middle of an otherwise healthy, growing colony of bacteria in which all growth activity has ceased for some "unknown" reason. Usually this death zone appears as a cleared area around an otherwise colored growth area. Initially it is an "abnormality" until further explanations become available; then, what was abnormal—when it happens again—becomes normal and accepted because now the "abnormality" is understood and can be anticipated in similar, future circumstances. (See Chapter Six and its footnote #5 for enlargement of these principles)

6. By far, most scientific discoveries have been made by trained and dedicated minds who literally stumble by chance (luck?) upon an unexpected phenomenon, such as Harvey Fire-

stone (1868–1938) in his "accidental" discovery of the synthetic process to make rubber.

Most solutions to laboratory criminal investigations are no exceptions since most start out as an enigma until a subtle, incomplete, impersonal clue ($+/-$) surfaces and is acted upon. This is not a game of chance nor an oversympathetic attitude for the victim since it involves not only proper identification, collection, and analyses of what is found but a reasonable extension of this information by synthesizing the data that is incompletely there or even "missing" from the otherwise normal event. Example: A + B = C is a long standing accepted principle in chemistry. The addition of two knowns (A and B) produce a predictable, expected known (C); (H + O = Water, H_2O). Conversely, if A is known and when mixed with B, a tentative unknown, if this combination produces the correct known compound C, then item B can be identified. Chemical crystal tests, double melting point and gas chromatography procedures are based on these principles which give confirmed, chemical derivatives. If correct assumptions were made initially, both "unknown" C and B can be anticipated with a very high degree of certainty.

Chapter 5

THE DISQUIET EVIDENCE

Nothing is more certain in modern society than the principle that there are no absolutes.

—Chief Justice Vincent
U.S. Supreme court

Men occasionally stumble over the truth but most of them pick themselves up and hurry off as if nothing had happened.

—Winston Churchill

We were working a night duty when a call came in from the dispatcher requesting the examination of a car thought to have possibly been involved in the hit-and-run death of a ten-year-old boy about a week before. Months of learning had now gone by since I first sat in a police car responding to a real (the heavy cases) crime scene. Now I was "on the chart" with rotating work shifts, however still as "the third wheel" on a two man team! This night was somewhat different and unusual in that I was filling in for a peer who was on vacation and a real team responded to this first request of the night, with me in the jump seat.

The car in question had been seized by the police because it met the general description given by witnesses. The accident had happened several nights before and witnesses had described it as a 1957 Chevrolet, deep dark in color (at night it could have been black, green, blue, et cetera). This car was black and had two of the license plate numbers mentioned by these viewers of the death scene. We had every reason to believe that the suspect car would have damage to its left front fender area from the description given. This car had a damaged front fender and a broken headlight, all on the left side! Glass fragments had been picked up at the scene of the accident, but little else.

Upon arriving at the location specified, the processing sequence began "by the numbers." Diagonal, front, and back photographs were taken with the car license plate in each view; ownership of the car was verified and the fact that the car had not been reported stolen established through the radio dispatcher. The interior of the car, of course, was dusted for latent prints! On the left front fender was noticed a rather large dent in and slightly over the leading edge of the car fender. With close observation and oblique lighting techniques, a thin, gray outline of a material impression could be seen inside the dented area. It appeared to be a light gray pattern of crossed fabric lines in the dust adhering to the fender of the vehicle. Due to the seriousness of this find and the difficulty of photographing this gray impression on a black background and the poor lighting apparatus available, the fender area was covered with a large piece of cardboard to protect the fragile image from accidental erasures. The car was driven back to the laboratory garage for closer inspection while the clothes worn by the dead boy were picked up from the local police precinct for direct comparisons under more controlled circumstances.

Within the large bag of evidence received from the police property room was a heavy sweater. The sweater, when distantly aligned to the plastic impression[1] in the car dent, was "obviously" the cause of this visible impression staring up at us. The thickness of the threads in both the image and the known sweater were similar, as was the thread count in both directions when the sweater was closely compared to the silhouette in the dark metal. Failing to obtain satisfactory photographs due to the small color contrast and zero depth of focus, the largest rubber lifts available, in both black and white, were used to soak up the image in the dent. The lifts could be more closely examined for a direct comparison to the sweater. There were indeed similar threads in the overall construction of the image and the sweater, but it failed to give the level of proof required by evidence for submission to a court of law. "The lifts contained no individualizing accidental characteristics when compared to the known specimen." This death as well as many others was almost unnoticed and certainly unheralded.

As analysts and as human beings, we felt like many drivers as they pass a loaded open truck, usually going in the opposite direction and the car windshield is hit with a shower of pebbles, at least one of which puts "a ding" in an otherwise undamaged glass windshield. You know who did it and how and when and where it was done; but try to prove it in a court of law. The feeling in the air was one of sheer frustration that could be cut with a knife! So close but yet so far.

Months later, in another serious case, the desirable accident was to elude us again!

A middle-aged homemaker was found dead on the floor of her kitchen with a knife protruding from her chest. The subsequent police investigation revealed that this mother of the family had spent the morning shopping in the area after sending her husband, who was a mechanic, off to work and her two children to school. Upon returning home, she found her second floor front apartment being burglarized in broad daylight. The police were summoned to this macabre scene by a neighbor who had stopped by to pass the time of day. The neighbor had found the front door of the apartment closed and locked but with the front door keys still in the outside lock.

When the police responded to the initial call, an immediate response reaction was called for on the part of these uniformed officers. During the ensuing shuffle and assault in the apartment, obvious from an overturned chair and broken glasses in the living room area, the struggle continued into the kitchen with table and chairs pushed aside and a canister of flour spilled onto a counter top and on to the kitchen floor. Clearly seen in this white debris on the floor were footprints as if in snow, in a twisting, dizzy, swirling overlapping pattern as their owners fought for control in a life threatening situation. From this muddled pattern, footprints in the image of a sneaker[2] slowly and quietly moved out of the kitchen to the rear door of the apartment, up two flights of stairs— two steps at a time—left, right; left, right. The white prints stopped in double formation as faint images in front of the fourth floor apartment rear door. The officers, following these impressions to their destination, rang the doorbell and were greeted by the mother of this lower middle-class home.

The officers, in justified zeal, inquired, "Do you have a son at home?"

"Yes!" she replied.

"Is he at home now?" one of the officers quickly asked in an even, monitored voice.

"No, he was home briefly but has gone out again."

The questioning continued as the group faced each other at the kitchen door. "Could we see your son's bedroom for a moment, ma'am?" they asked.

"I don't see why not, if you will only take a few minutes. I am cooking an early supper," she replied.

The woman of the home permitted the officers entrance and the inspection desired. On the floor of the son's closet was a pair of sneakers with white powder on them, the powder impressed into the indentations and corners on the bottom of each sneaker. Serendipity had struck again.

"If you don't mind," the officers said in determined voice and mannerism, "we'll need to take these sneakers and leave an officer here to meet your boy when he returns home." The sneakers were safeguarded and given to the detective in charge of the case and the boy taken to the local police station for questioning upon his return home some forty-five minutes later.

The crime scene field team from the crime laboratory arrived after being summoned in the routine manner, when the police dispatcher initially mobilized the department's homicide response system. Again, photographs of the overall general area were immediately taken along with specific pictures of the kitchen and close-up photos "with rulers in place" were taken of the several white plastic footprints in the floor. The rooms were dusted for latent fingerprints, blood samples were dutifully taken from the walls and floor when found. These all were identified, noted and preserved as required. The "point of entry" was established as the scene was processed and pieces of the puzzle came together. It was a "step-over burglary." The perpetrator gained entrance to the apartment by climbing out a public stairwell, hall window, and stepped over to the adjacent open living room window with a fall of two floors to a concrete yard if he lost his balance. This was not an unusual method of entry used by agile youths who had little knowledge of burglary methods but a lot of daring and a minimum sense of the danger present, especially at higher levels. The location of the dining room window, without any nearby fire escape or other supports gave the homeowners a false sense of security and this window was often left ajar in warm weather. This method became a good, fast point of entry to the premises for those who knew of this peculiarity and for those who had a dare to do.

Many fortuitous alternatives had taken place and were accidentally in place when the flour was spilled on to the kitchen floor. The shoeprints lead the police to the perpetrator directly. Had the flour not been spilled, the "point of exit" of the perpetrator would not have been so obvious. Had the perpetrator gone down the rear stairs to the street, instead of up, the plastic impressions would have shown the direction of escape but little else once the offender gained access to the public area of the city streets. Had the aggressor not taken two steps at a time going up the stairs, the flour would have been deposited on twice as many stairs and been depleted well short of apartment 403. Had the invader not changed his sneakers or had he gone to a higher level in the eight-story apartment, the accusing flour would most probably have again been depleted long before the footprints arrived at their destination, either to another safe dwelling or to the roof; out, over, and down to a distant, unknown location. Had any of these possible events occurred, the frustrations so often experienced in these situations would have set in sooner.

The laboratory field team quickly retreated back to "the house" with their gold mine of material evidence and the associated knowledge and information. Here, a mountain of technical problems arose!

The pictures of the sneakers marching out the door at the rear of the apartment, all developed well, qualitatively and quantitatively. However, when the sneakers became immersed in the flour, the individual accidental identifying characteristics present in most footwear (abrasions implanted into the heel and sole areas from normal use against debris in the street) were obliterated due to the abundant source of flour. (Too much of a good thing.) The fact that flour was found in the open design spaces of the sneakers was considered incidental to any individualizing identification process. The shuffling of two sets of feet dancing around during the continued assault destroyed any "positive cast" that might have been present. The footprints walking away from the scene clearly showed gross sneaker images. By the time enough flour had fallen off to begin to expose the needed accidentals in the sneakers, the footprints had reached uneven rear wooden platforms, stairs, and stairwell. The prints could be clearly seen mounting the steps one on every other step, but on top of black, worn, rubber stair pads, any accidentals were lost from view. Most certainly, some vital information was also lost when the first uniformed police officers rushed up the same back stairs in their timely pursuit of the perpetrator. A tease to say the least! The evidence was there and it loudly mocked us!

It was as easy to envision who did the killing and walked in the sneakers as it was to follow, first the positive plastic shoe prints and then the latent sneaker impressions, gradually fading only to stop at apartment 403, but how was the laboratory to prove it in a court of law without the needed individualizing accidentals that had become fugitive? Once again, a shallow report was written. "The sneaker imprints were similar to the submitted items but contained insufficient individual characterizations for identification." A meaningless, weightless report almost worse than none at all because we were unable to deal with the technical imperfections in the evidence due to a psychic denial of otherwise self-evident truths in the factual situation. The fact that there was flour on the floor of the death scene and in the crevices of both sneakers was treated as an *accidental coincidence* and any cause and effect relationship, if understood, was avoided.

The shoes themselves were excluded under exclusionary search and seizure court procedures. The police lacked a search warrant and upon entering the apartment in good faith and even with permission, the case had progressed from an investigatory process over to an accusatory mode and on finding the sneakers in the closet a search warrant was needed. Not having had it, the sneakers were excluded from court presentation and the case dismissed! The police "were there to investigate and not to assist the accused," which is a legal mark of distinction. Any credibility attached to the "hot pursuit" principle was inappropriate.

The failure "in the laboratory" was equally obvious because serendipity had worked both sides of the street in the same case. It produced the chance flour impressions (positive and plastic) and then obliterated the needed, fragile, and fugitive accidentals (if they were there) in a fickle fated situation. We were once again mere puppets of circumstances. Certainly not unwilling to do the job, to do anything that needed to be done; but what was it that eluded us? It seemed to plague us! Collectively we were good at grasping at smoke!

A reasonable contact with reality had eluded us and somehow the rights of the victims become all mixed up in this legal and technical mumbo jumbo as the system collectively transgressed the canons of common sense. The courts have set up barriers primarily to protect and prevent a second innocent victim, the accused, from having his civil rights disregarded unless a jury said otherwise. These barriers were not too high that they were impossible to overcome but there have to be *concerted efforts* from the prosecution side of the case to do it and these efforts have to be right and according to law. The criminal courts do strive for utmost fairness to the accused when a trial has commenced. The judges are, in fact, at this stage in the game, biased referees in the defendant's favor; the judges' position is not to hang the guilty but to protect the possible innocent person against unjustified state intrusion into the personal life of the accused. The accused is and at all times remains innocent under law even if under the worst of circumstances when an innocent person would be expected to shout loudly to protect his innocence, but remains mute. The accused does not have to "take the stand" in his own defense nor can he be forced to testify against himself regardless of the circumstances or the violence associated with the crime. No inference can be made by the prosecution at trial, to the jury, of this silence. The prosecution is and must always be in the position to prove its credibility in each case using corroboration and reasonableness in any single item of evidence and in the total overall aggregate of the evidence presented in each case. The burden is always on the state to prove "beyond a reasonable doubt"[3] (never beyond an overwhelming doubt) that the defendant is guilty in the minds of his peers, the jury. It is they, after all, who have the unequal and burdensome responsibility to see through the smoke.

I know justice is blind as she weighs the evidence in her balances and I know all too well the individual accidentals that can be present in shoe prints that these objective experts are so diligently looking for and that these accidentals are not there in this case. The flour prints are there and so is the poor old lady on the kitchen floor, never to move or laugh or cry again. The evidence, with its predictable expectations as stark reality, is staring us in the face, leading us, if we will follow the inductive route, right into the perpetrators' bedroom! Nothing could be stronger evidence, except a signed confession in triplicate, than these compelling observations. I know all too well, even when we do get footprints with more than "the damnable twelve points of identification" many examiners are still hesitant because we do not know who was actually wearing the sneakers at the time of the crime (shades of Lizzie Borden).[4] This again is secular humanism at its worst; telling those who will listen—and there are many who have—not to take their consciences, morality, or any ethics into the work place (court room) with them because to do so will upset or ruin long established policies that were developed to cover all contingencies. The possibility that such comprehensive policies could never be developed is never questioned. The victims of criminal violence personally pay for this delinquent attitude when these established policies do fail to meet the victims' needs when their cases do not reach a predetermined, high analytical level of acceptance. Such cases never reach a court of law for trial. This whole field of criminalistics is one sad, expensive joke on the taxpayer and the victim. We have to find a way to overcome this organizational impairment and give these inductive artifacts and our consciences an unmuffled voice in order to stop this prolonged injustice. The victims, their civil rights having been violated, cannot cry out to make their needs heard and the evidence that could reconcile the wrong and bring retribution is there, pointing the way, but is unheard and unseen. How can this need go on unanswered when it is so obvious? The implicit reasonableness and internal demand would be obvious to a twelve-year-old child using minimum common sense. As we get older, we must lose this capability, retreat from our responsibilities, deny the reality that seems to be heard but into deaf ears.

The responses to the questions are as hard to fathom as is

the solution to the technical necessities that elude us! There is always a void, a chasm, a riddle that separates us from a meaningful solution, because the imperfect evidence seen in this case should never be considered as nebulous or irrelevant or as a casual link, but a direct congruence, a working consensus that acknowledges a compelling precedence of intrinsic worth as a progenitor with the virtue of consistency as is seen in nature. One thing is for sure, unless we willingly accept responsibility, initiative, and the risk to carry the burden, to act as intercessors and petitioners for the victims, the crucial main link in the evidence will be as anemic as any dead fish and will not be given over for jury review. Isn't this the true essence of criminalistics, to interdict with the imperfect evidence, to make the truth known to a jury of our peers, to put the cards on the table as God gives us the means to do so, and let the jury worry about it? I will have done my job—let them do theirs! With all their instruments, no mere chemist will do this because there is no place to hide; even their precious charts are not big enough for that now. To both chemists and criminalists alike, let it be known that we now are what we each want to be, but the more important point of consideration is, are we both in the correct profession? Can we both stay in criminalistics? I think not for the victim's sake, if for no other. Only an authentic criminalist would acknowledge the logical and necessary existence of the "invisible" components, the intrinsic interdependence, the lasting predictable associations, the irresistible combinations, the demand characteristics, that are present in so many of these imperfect cases. We must find a way to give the authentic criminalist and the incomplete evidence "a voice" to do so. We must not continue to perpetuate these mistakes by ceasing to ignore the obvious and become more concerned for doing what is right than fearing a wrong, thereby demonstrating some competitive gristle in our court testimony.

To be fair to all concerned, what has happened is that a conflict, a mismatch has occurred that mutes the reproaches of logic and common sense. A professional chemist actually works in a crime laboratory isolated from the more miscellaneous, less professional factors, whereas an authentic criminalist as the proactive expert state witness involved in a criminal, advocatory, legal system cannot operate in such a vacuum isolated from the dynamics of a suffering, blind, human, organic, destitute criminal investigation in which any imperfect evidence is disregarded and then discarded. The authentic criminalist is as vital a necessity to the proper functioning of the system as salt is to food, blood is to the whole body, as a flower is to a rosebush. To a chemist, the "happy occurrences," these serendipitous findings are intolerable, irritating, distressing voids in his scientific, professional investigation. No reassuring consistencies are even noted. An authentic criminalist notices these same aberrations as natural, expected, empty spaces in an equally ordered, interlocking system that requires an initator like himself, who is reality-adjusted, a compassionate interpreter to diagnose and decode this same "enigma" by methodizing his education, training, experience, expectations, and faithfully extrapolating these candid realizations to an empaneled jury for *their* consideration and judgment. He has no interest in being just a quality control chemist who possesses only selective sight—presenting to a jury only those cases that can be proven "beyond a scientific doubt" and within "zero error" limitations and reject all others of less character.

The chemist and the criminalist each have a personal agenda, but the criminalist, far more than the chemist, can meet the needs of the victims of criminal violence and those of the criminal courts, since it is he who must set up a meaningful agenda for argument. Only when this has been accomplished has the concerned expert fulfilled his obligation by dealing with true reality in each criminal case—at the crucial site—"where the tire meets the roadway." Only the authentic criminalist will respond to the essential reality in each situation and be able to deal with the multiple variables constantly present in almost all criminal cases.

Only in this manner may one promote dialogue with reality by admitting to a conscience coherent pattern of arrangements in the evidence that is almost telepathic and fatalistic to the perpetrator(s). It will take more than just a change in metaphor (chemist to criminalist); that alone will not make a bad idea good. The mechanical horror of "zero error" and analysis "proven beyond a scientific doubt" and other vulgar avoidance strategies must be replaced. We must develop an inner, more open logic; a willingness and courage to risk, in order to serve the truth and the victims of criminal violence. In this search a margin of error must be anticipated and pondered. Administrative policies that encourage us to express the deeply felt demands, the visceral twinge, must be developed. Criminalistics and the law are applied sciences, not stale theories, and they require practical maxims reflecting an intricate latticework, not counsels of perfection, as sufficient guides to action. The banality in crime laboratory reports is a source of embarrassment since such uninspired, evasive reporting is less devoted to the real truth than to intellectual vacuity and nonsense. Such reports stand all our worldly standards of reasonableness and common sense on their heads and common sense and our sense of justice rebels. These inquiries are not flat or one-sided but shout at you and are insistent, but go unheard because few will take the risk to allow it to be otherwise. In so many cases, the disquieting reality—the aggregate truth—is so close you can actually touch it. Very few chemists will do what needs to be done, and few notice that it is not done, and the case is marked "closed."

How can we view these crimes without bleeding a little inside? Such strong sentiment is vicious banality if it suffices as our total commitment, if we do not strongly oppose the march of these events. Such silence must be viewed as condescension masquerading as compassion that only produces a crippling rationalization which deflates initiative and makes any effort feeble especially when such passivity brings rewards and promotions.

Are we not evading the demands of truth when we deny these experiences of value? Why struggle with this reality when that is held in such little regard? Only those concerned with the victims can stimulate the positive struggle to support those in need and not suffocate the effort.

MEANINGFUL DISCLOSURES

1. A forensic term to describe various impressions that can be found at crime scenes.

A plastic print or impression would resemble an impression that could be seen if one placed one finger on a tab of butter or in oil, leaving a visible impression. Such images can be noticed with prints produced by body oils or prints seen in drops or smears of blood, dust, or tar; shoe prints and tire impressions as seen in mud or snow. No extra effort other than just looking is required to see the impression.

A latent print or impression requires artificial development, using powders or chemicals to see or to make visible the otherwise invisible impression. Prior to processing a surface, these latent prints, unlike the plastic prints, cannot be seen by the unaided eye.

2. The flour, acting as a white ink pad, had saturated the soles of the sneakers and the sneakers became a stamper.

3. Never beyond an overwhelming doubt or even to a scientific doubt.

4. A homicide case of some note that occurred early in this century. Only two people were present in the home at the time of the occurrence. One was a maid and the other, Lizzie Borden, was the daughter and as a family member had full and unencumbered access to the premises. A double killing occurred on the premises two hours apart with "no witnesses" except these two occupants of the home. The trial jury found Miss Borden innocent of the criminal charges against her. It seems that the jury would

not convict on the basis of the law of substraction (a forced decision which is their prerogative), the smoking gun principle, nor consider the emphatic probability that was before their eyes and make the legitimate leap in logic that seems to have been required. In the opinion of some, the author included, Miss Borden was the only one who had the desire, means, and opportunity to perform the crime. Since there were no other witnesses to the act and a weak prosecution, Miss Borden was released and the two victims forever left wanting for justice and retribution. As an acquitted defendant she could never again be accused with the crime. No one else was ever charged with the felony.

Chapter 6

MASTERING THE FUNDAMENTALS

The law is the most complex of all sciences and cannot be expected to reach the icy stratosphere of certainty.

—Chief Justice Charles Evans Hughes
U.S Supreme Court

An expert need not have absolute certitude about his opinion for it to be considered and allowed into evidence in a court of law.

—U.S. vs. Wilson'
(441–F2d 655, 1971)

—Dyas vs. U.S.
(376A.2D827, 1977)

—State vs. Washington
(622 P.2D 968, 1981)

Having been driving for over two hours and having been up since 5:00 A.M. for the administrative meeting in Phoenix, the driver of the white patrol car has been on the go for some fifteen hours, almost nonstop. The driver slows the car to a stop on the right shoulder of the road so he can enjoy a respite and the cup of coffee that has been waiting to be consumed since the stop at Indian Junction many miles to the south. There is little concern for safety in parking the car in this manner although the night is so dark. The passing traffic in both directions forms two moving streams of light on the otherwise darkened highway—the red lights going north and the white ribbon going south. Under other circumstances this might be a nice place to take a nap but sleep is out of the question because the memories continue through the driver's bewildered mind as it continues to recall and be affected by so many memories—the different criminal cases. His reminiscing continues.

We all come from different neighborhoods, but the normal routines of various family units give the various areas deep similarities. The daily family activities duplicate themselves in a very predictable manner throughout any given week. Reflecting this almost constant routine, most family units often require the presence of a babysitter from some neighbor's home to care for dependent children when the parents find the time for some needed relaxation.

On that summer Thursday night, a neighbor requested a local teenager to baby-sit a three-year-old while the young couple enjoyed a night out celebrating their fourth wedding anniversary. The young coed was experienced at this friendly chore, having performed the task for several years with many neighbors and with many repeats. The young girl is almost eighteen years old, with a thin build and a well-kept appearance. It is doubtful she will be able to go on to college due to family financial problems, although academically she is well suited for the challenge. She arrives at her neighbors' home at the proper time and the young couple depart for a pleasant evening. For the young baby-sitter this evening will be more enjoyable to her than most because the young couple has a color TV and a VCR with a good size library to pick from and a full refrigerator.

The evening in this home passed quietly in this laid back part of town until a knock was heard at the door. Upon answering this summons the young girl saw that it was her ex-boyfriend. The two youths had been schoolmates for many years and they had been going together for several months and he had been her ex several times. It was a friendly encounter.

What exactly transpired after the door was closed will always be conjecture. The facts as pieced together hours later by the police leave many gaps, none of which would change the ultimate outcome.

The young couple returned home several hours later than had been originally anticipated. The young husband remained in the family car to quickly take the baby-sitter home while his wife entered the home to alert the young girl that her extended work period was ended. The mother was the first to notice the strange scene as she entered through the front door. The home was lighted as usual but the coed was nowhere to be found. The mother immediately went to the small room off the master bedroom to check the condition of her infant son. He was quietly sleeping in an otherwise empty house. She rushed out of the house to alert her waiting husband to the circumstances she had found. Upon entering, the couple searched the home more closely. In the rear family TV room was found a strange large wet red stain in the rug. There were smears of red liquid on the kitchen floor that they followed to the rear steps of the house. Not knowing what had occurred, but with sufficient information to be alarmed, the young husband called the police and the coed's parents. Within a few minutes the police arrived, followed some twenty minutes later by the coed's concerned parents.

It was easy enough to follow the red stains out the rear door because there were so many of them. It appeared that someone was badly hurt and was being dragged for some unknown reason. The steps leading down from a rear porch were stained red as was the gravel path for some forty feet, which led to a small stream used by the locals as a fishing area. Additional police assistance arrived and a search of the river bank was begun with emphasis downstream. It took all of two hours for the police to find the coed's body, caught in the branches of a fallen tree partially obstructing the waterway, less than a mile away. The girl was dead, fully clothed but badly beaten.

In most areas of the country the local police perform all the required tasks with one officer designated as the crime scene investigator when the occasion requires that he be reassigned from traffic duty or other assignments. Having this capability, it is said, gives these departments the independence and the spontaneity needed and the lines of authority are short, clear, and uncluttered. The problem, if anyone was to admit that there was a problem, was that the "crime scene officer" usually does not have much experience processing this type of a scene since he has only seen a few other homicide cases in the last five years. The professionals at the state crime laboratory located some distance away see many more such cases in a much shorter period of time but "they are there and we are here" and "we can handle our own" —so say the local police officials. The crime scene is processed, photographs taken, witnesses interviewed, autopsy performed and all the proper notifications made "by the book."

About a week later, the state crime laboratory received a large carton, by personal delivery from the "crime scene officer" now acting in the capacity of a "property custodian". This fifteen-man department was a fully developed agency and its detectives were following every clue that was developed by them at the scene. The articles of evidence now being delivered was the sum of their efforts and they expected something meaningful from the crime laboratory personnel.

The fifty-seven articles of evidence submitted to the crime laboratory were all properly labeled and packaged and the chain of evidence was well established. However, the reception of so many articles of evidence sometimes indicates the small amount of serious decision making that was performed at the scene by these professionals. The large box of evidence was culled by the appropriate members of the laboratory and twenty-eight items were eventually identified to have a preliminary, positive reaction for the presence of blood, the benzidine reagent having given its proper quick purple color reaction on each item tested. The analyst in the serology section who was assigned the case was one of the more competent, dedicated individuals "to come down the pike" in some time. The normal blood testing procedures for typing, cross matching, and species identification of the individual samples were correctly performed.

Six weeks of effort produced a final serology report that indicated in some detail that the twenty-eight items were examined for the presence of blood; twenty-eight times the various samples of evidence were described in the report which monotonously noted that each item contained samples of human blood, having the blood type of A positive. A good technical analysis was performed on each item and a high mark for proficiency would have been obtained had these tests been performed in any academic atmosphere. There was no incompleteness in this report—all the details were there. The immediate problem was that the contiguity in the compelling, biased evidence was not noted! There had been no attempt to use any statistical, representative sampling techniques on these items from a single homicide scene as a dependable forecasting scheme, nor were any other similarly situated cases exposed to this reasoning method. It had taken six weeks to establish that the blood on the twenty eight items was human blood, type A positive. No mention, correlation or discussion was made in the report that the blood type was at least similar to the deceased. A five minute phone call to the local medical examiner's officer could have verified this coed's blood type (known sample from autopsy) was also A positive. No consideration is given to the fact that if any five randomly selected evidence samples in the case had been tested and if the same results were obtained from each of the specimens a very high and reasonable probability would exist, predicting that the other twenty-three mutually exclusive items would have also been human blood type A positive. Would it have been an unreasonable stretch of the imagination to then reasonably predict that all the stains belonged to the deceased? I would hope not—but this was/is never attempted—"it's unprofessional," almost vulgar to deal with these unpalatable facts. (This and the resulting backlog of cases that constantly plague most crime laboratories would never have happened if the nation's crime laboratories were employed in private industry where a higher emphasis for effectiveness is an important factor.) This final report was a decision without insight; an objective, unproductive indifference, a benevolent neutrality to the built-in statistical premise and to the expected activity of a prosecution expert. It was/is a serious attempt for the "professional criminalist" to stay away from life's messier realities.[2] The sole purpose of such testing was devoured by the process and no one took notice that no correction no opinion/convictions of the predictable expectations in the evidence was ever expressed in the written reports sent to court.[3]

From a practical viewpoint, sheer reflective experience and repeated verifications (process recording) indicates that the blood found at any single homicide scene belongs to the victim and to no others. Having been involved in well over four hundred homicide investigations in over twenty years in the profession, this author has never experienced (nor heard of) a homicide case where the perpetrator was seriously injured at the scene (single or multiple homicide)! There have been instances where the sole survivor indicates to the police that he was injured by an unknown perpetrator (such descriptions are always vague) but without exception, the injuries and the associated blood loss are slight and not life threatening and are seriously thought (found) to be self-inflicted; the injuries being superficial when compared to the injuries received by any of the deceased. A false story has been concocted to confuse the issues and shift the concentration of the police investigators to others.

Likewise in narcotic cases, where at times, huge, voluminous amounts of similarly packaged items are submitted for analysis, complete testing of all individual items is also performed without any attempt to make insightful decisions. The contiguity that is in the evidence is ignored again.

If a case of 500 glassine envelopes is sent to a crime laboratory from a police agency (each envelope containing a white or similar powder or similar pills, capsules, or tablets having the same color or shape), present procedures require that all 500 items be completely and individually tested. Basic reason would seem to indicate that if 50 envelopes are randomly selected and completely tested and if all 50 proved to be the same drug, there then is a high probability, a high correlation coefficient and consequently a high predictability that the remaining 450 envelopes are also the same drug. If even one of the initial 50 envelopes (pills, capsules or tablets) proves to be different, then all 500 would then need to be tested in order to maintain the same confidence factor. This statistical sampling of these items of evidence is completely rejected by the vast majority of experts.

They place little confidence in the technique and even less value on the existence of a permanent essence in the group tested.

To the credit of some laboratories, this technique has been attempted on rare occasions only to have the misunderstanding arise and root itself in the prosecutor's office or strongly objected to by the defense attorney in court. These various officials need to learn to work with statistical sampling techniques. Many attorneys accept that for reasons of expediency, this procedure would be acceptable but that only the 50 envelopes completely tested be allowed into evidence for consideration of the court and the jury. All concerned know all too well that the total weight of the narcotic seized and accepted in court has a direct bearing on the length of sentence given after conviction; the fewer admitted into evidence the lighter the sentence. This is a self-serving, absolute denial, and rejection of the well-established principle in statistical random sampling and the high predictability inherent in the technique. All 500 envelopes really were tested when the 50 envelopes (pills, capsules, or tablets) were randomly selected and tested. This is the threshold problem in that the decisions rendered are based only on objective, exogenous information and regretfully, this is the only permissible game in town—absentminded automatism! It is an effort to work in an advocatory system of justice but in a frictionless manner. The analyses conducted are as cosmetic as they are real because there are no risks involved in the analyses sent to court and this places a cloud over and gives momentum to the impossibility of developing any incentive for independent fact finding ability in the individual examiner on the more demanding cases.[4] If these unbelievers were correct in their dogmatic and insensitive beliefs, no blood analysis could be attempted at a hospital from just a few drops of the red liquid taken from a patient's finger; no spectral analysis of any metal or chemical test could be attempted without consuming the entire item; no one would know they were eating an apple until it was fully consumed. The potent, built-in reality in these procedures, that nature cries out for order and synthesis is blatantly ignored. The profession of scientific jurisprudence (criminalistics) is in desperate need of a shot of testosterone to overcome our demonstrated inabilities to deal with these unpleasant realities that are present in all our incidental learning processes.

If these and other seemingly diverse circumstances are not sensibly addressed as serious, endogenous, integrated concerns in the overall central failure of crime laboratories to respond to the needs of the victims of criminal violence, a very critical flaw will have been overlooked to the severe detriment of all those concerned with justice. Those who do not accept the latter inductive, investigative, integrative procedures in criminal cases do not hear the appeal to conscience that these cases and many lesser ones hold within them. In either case, there is a lasting negative resonance effect to the act the consequences of which go far beyond the obvious and is schismatic between a chemist and a criminalist; the former has become a value free agent, a fair weather reporter, who refuses to express the logical consequences (an intelligent subjectivity) in the evidence because he is easily satisfied with the instant gratification of being a chemist while the latter hears the pleas in these cases and responds by further integrating the incomplete evidence for jury consideration after accepting the professional hazards involved. To the degree that the chemist desires to eliminate these professional risks, there is a loss in the ability to develop creative intervention with any "new" but imperfect evidence. The very basic theme is to determine if justice is the mere object of our search (the impersonal it) or the subject of our search (the personal, internalized I - you). Some otherwise inescapable implications will be missed if no such subjectivity and reasonableness is utilized.

Under ideal conditions the evidence developed from any criminal case should be complete with all the required accidentals and precise reactions and information conveniently available to a neophyte analyst. However, this is a simplistic fallacy since under realistic conditions with the exception of blood and bulk narcotic cases, such utopian expectations are always fallacious. In the vast majority of all other criminal cases, the analyst will be forced to work with incomplete, circumstantial evidence certainly less than we would like—and less than the very best. Every perpetrator of any crime will of course try to avoid leaving any trace of himself at the scene. He will flee whenever possible and deny all involvement in the incident. His civil rights will be protected—before, during, and after any indictment or required court appearances. If, therefore, conflicting professional priorities (isomers or analogs)[5] or inappropriate naive responses to the myriad of evidential pieces of evidence that can be found in these cases are permitted to develop early in the professional career of prosecution expert (laboratory) analysts, unsuitably high analytical bench marks will be forever established in his mind. As experts for the prosecution we will have assumed inappropriate responsibilities for trying to prove every existing item in a case or the absence thereof since the analyst is permitted to become enmeshed in peripheral considerations that have little material usefulness to the solution of the criminal case. This is more properly a defense responsibility, tactic, and ploy. These purist but unnecessary activities will be almost impossible to change as the analyst matures[6] and is promoted into other complicated disciplines that require even more risk in the decision-making process. The more difficult and unpleasant situations will be conveniently avoided by most professional analysts as they refuse to step out of bounds into the critical areas, especially if there is no managerial encouragement to accept and deal with risks as an inherent job related presumption.

The professional analyst so produced will place his analytical needs, philosophy, and intellectual pride above the needs of the victims and not seek reasonable interventions with the incomplete evidence that most often are the only artifacts found at a crime scene. Such reasonable compromise is, of course, always situational, which requires personal involvement, except in modern day crime laboratory reporting, which continually flinches from confrontation with debatable reality with its precarious aspects. If these inductive reasoning processes and associated risks are unacceptable in conventional narcotic and serology analyses, the failure in not discerning the real potentials, the tight couplings, the strategic and dynamic connections, the continuities in these simple but imperfect situations will materially contribute to much larger penetration failures in the more serious cases. If there is no consideration to what is predictable in the exhaustive evidence cases (blood and narcotics) there can be no recognition of or response to the unpredictable find when it is stumbled upon in the more unresolved cases. These many small failures in minor cases, the stiff standardized procedures that ignore the meaningful coordinates, the pragmatic alternatives under controlled conditions, will severely prevent a learning process to mature. An analyst, possessing this technical bias of not accepting or properly using statistical representative sampling techniques, intuitive probability projections, or their reservoir of experiences as viable meaningful methods to identify truth, to recapture the reality by expressing the probative values (in the imperfect evidence) the factual situation, is myopically preoccupied and insensitive to his responsibilities and those of a crime laboratory.

An authentic criminalist will express these probative values in the imperfect evidence and not obliterate the moral distinctions present. Failing to do this, the fainthearted analyst continuously works with severe disadvantages when trying to interpret other more latent unlocking realizations when present in evidence received from any other crime scene (case). He is keeping his eye on the hole in the donut instead of concentrating on the donut. This passivity is very widespread in the technical community that serves the criminal justice system and this severely limits the police from meeting their responsibilities to these same victims in our advocatory system of justice! The chemists who have been working in criminalistics are caught between their ethical principles and their professional interests and they have chosen to follow their interests and in doing so are guilty of lying by omission to the courts. In doing so these workers have accepted the counsel for perfection, when it is known that in reality there is no perfection anywhere, at any time. The problem is the denial of this fundamental reality by either overspecialization with no personal accountability and little managerial coordination of these experts or misplaced and mismatched specialization by professional chemists who should not be working in criminalistics. An authentic criminalist must use his education, training, and experiences along with reasonable, inductive logic and relevant imagery to breathe life and meaning into the evidence and the artifacts found in criminal evidence and not be so organizationally impaired. Such weighted values in terms of subjective probability will materially assist the police and the juries, both of whom are hungry for it. This is critical thinking that is renounced by professional chemists working in criminalistics. It is, however, very germane for all criminalists to correlate and assimilate the stiff idealistic chemical platitudes with everyday reality and go beyond the level of easy fulfillment and interpolate our imperfect findings to the criminal courts. We must not substitute energy and mechanical proficiency for reason and valued judgments. No longer will new problems and new circumstances be covered over by old static answers. If an inductive system of reasonableness and a graduated, proportional response to latent potentials in the evidence can be developed (expert-intuitive-subjective-analytical probability), we will be able to penetrate and come to terms with the ever-changing cases as they really are, not as we would professionally like them to be.

The old answers are an attempt to modify or disregard reality and its logical implications and if it does not fit a preset theoretical or analytical template it is discarded. That which is discarded doesn't count and is not counted statistically or in any other way. That which is discounted and discarded suffers a drastically diminished reality. Somehow we must develop a broader prism range that is not tolerant of simple yes or no decisions. It is not a matter of being right or wrong or having sufficient accidentals in any pattern (points of identity, crystal tests, confirmatory tests without number, adequate spectra, or signed confessions) as it is to be relevant to the events and to the victims innocently caught up in these inimical scenes. Instinctive morality or reflective ethics demands that we deal more meaningfully with these events.

We criminalists must raise above the self-sufficient isolation of pat answers and protective traditions into a hyperawareness of the human need existing in these victims. All that can be said now is that we are not happy with the programmed results we have seen because it would mean we are blind to the obvious. Truly seeing is a painful thing but the pain will be worth experiencing in order to overcome our own sheltered ignorance and to express the honesty seen in these tight associations. It is also a statement of love, honor, and solidarity with the victim. What we propose to develop is an argument from conscience that goes where the action is—where it is needed; such reform from within is always a heavy labor whether it is in the laboratory or in a court of law. We cannot continue to have purpose devoured by process!

An authentic criminalist is a person who occupationally inherits the obligation to organize, interpret through evaluative judgments the relevant information gathered from articles of evidence so that it can be evaluated by a jury of our peers. There is nothing mechanical (like some inventory schedule), linear, or totally objective in the efforts expended to recreate specific circumstances into a coherent framework from disjointed information viewed as narrow, isolated, an inventory of variables. A criminalist needs to use both logic and intution, recognize both facts and feelings, have a comprehension of the nonverbal, have a visual imagination and perspective; be both a technically competent and emotionally caring individual whose fondness for science is allied to reason. This individual's decisions are based on a conviction developed through penetrating observations and comprehensive integration of the developed evidence. The evidence perused, although incomplete, has predictive values (nature's regularities), procured from mutations of our experiences, an intersubjective understanding (the normal vs. the abnormal) seen as a process awareness, which were established from previous truths (process recordings). A compassionate yet strong and wise criminalist attempts to reconcile realistic truth with cognitive truth (good judgment) making eclectic judgments. His discipline allows him to develop the ability to make necessary concessions and not remain technically paranoid. He has an ethical and moral if not legal obligation to be proactive for the victims of violent crimes, when through his efforts the truth is revealed for jury consideration. Such criminalists are effective chemists since they are not tied down to unproductive, prepackaged, preprocessed activities that tend to substitute procedures and learned behaviors for substance. Both the chemist and the criminalist are victims of their previous successes but a criminalist utilizes his tests as interface filters between the evidence and the final report not as compulsive, ritualistic ends in themselves as a chemist seems to use his objective instrumentation. The traditional criminalist finds evidence of reason in his analysis and can express this inner excitement, the expectation of this order, as a probability. The chemist visualizes no inherent necessity in this sequence nor believes in its repeatability. Criminalists in most cases cannot prove to the limits of certainty that a catastrophe will not occur tomorrow in Seattle but there is a very high probability that such will not happen tomorrow or in the foreseeable future. This is the normal extrapolation of past experiences into the future, and a process upon which we all live our daily lives. Basically, the criminalist makes an ethical choice in his differential analysis that appears to be reasonably in agreement with reality, is within the court given guidelines, and poses no contradiction to, but support for, our jury system of justice.

To deliberately, through hesitation or restraint, subvert our advocatory system of law is a severe contradiction to our area of specialization within the criminal justice system. At the heart of the process is the search for truth! If this search is not realized to the greatest extent possible, the jury, as agents of the general will, cannot perform their duties as triers of the facts and the victims are left wanting. Experts, in a variety of ways, can frustrate this process through bias, information overload, a passion for certainty,[7] or by preempting the jury's decision-making role. To continue to explicitly do so is a strain that can cut us off from other important avenues of consideration, completely frustrating justice and the search for truth. To avoid such reflections, to be approval oriented will lose a vital dimension in advocacy process. For some reason, we have not been bold enough, realistic enough, or imaginative enough to examine in detail the pressures on the state's expert's decision-making process and the medium in which these decisions are made. To date these areas have been inaccessible and are areas with which few argue or wrestle. We have been a privileged cadre of cosmopolitan critics, far too removed from the turmoil of these crimes, which has allowed us to discretely walk away from the situation if perfect circumstances do not present themselves.

As criminalists, we are not independent contractors but members of a complex, multifunctional, mutually dependent, interactive, diagnostic system, culminating in the recreating of reality for jury consideration. There seems to be little agreement, reasoning, or inference that the many submitted articles of evidence are not arbitrary, that the natural law is in effect and working, that actions and situations are not static but are interactive, dependent, interlinked variables, each a part of a yet undiscovered whole. We must not apply the insensitive scientific model too rigidly and become obsessed with investigating facts rather than functional relationships. Our expressed opinions are ventures into realism that must endure uncertainty as an occupational hazard and are expressed as guided, reasonable projections revealing the latent truth. In doing so, the motive to use the suggested overreaching vision (intuitive probability) is to transcend the rhetoric and our unpalatable predispositions that to date have been so inadequate in expressing the latent truth. This expert knows that he will "never have all the pieces of the puzzle" that others require before making his decisions. His quest is to consider the preponderance of the evidence, establish necessary significant connections and risk error in his search for the truth that is always subject to jury review. To do otherwise will result in a severe loss of vital information for the jury, and the loss from this travesty of justice for the victims almost exceeds our capacity for indignation. These deflections from the norm to the implicit order must be noticed and expressed (as per Locard, Fleming, and so many others) or the nation's citizens could lose their faith and hope in the criminal justice system to which, some day, almost all of us will need to appeal.

MEANINGFUL DISCLOSURES

1. This unrecognized court decision is as relative to proactive criminalists as is the Good Samaritan Law to medical doctors.

Heretofore, medical doctors passing a scene of a serious accident refused to give aid because the street scene was a totally inappropriate locale for medical practice since it lacked the standard and necessary sanitary conditions and medical equipment for the rendering of responsible and *professional* medical intervention that is incumbent upon them to do. Many people unnecessarily died at these scenes until the role of the medical provider and the awkward problems he faced at these contaminated scenes were more clearly defined.

This court decision not only gives court experts guidance and direction but anticipates the existence of incomplete/imperfect criminal evidence and makes appropriate allowances so that the hidden agendas in the evidence can be revealed for judicial review. See Chapter Fourteen and its footnote #5.

2. See Chapter Two and its footnote #1 and Chapter Nine and its footnote #1.

3. The expected correlation was evaded by both the analyst and by crime laboratory management. It would appear that it is more important for the analyst to demonstrate his technical versatility than to assist the police in solving the crime.

4. It is postured that to be a decent criminal court expert one must use both deductive and inductive (integrated, professional common sense) thinking processes and reject any reference to the Nuremberg Defense ("I was doing my job as ordered") if justice for the victims of criminal violence is bungled. Intelligent subjectivity will prevent this from occurring. See Chapter Fourteen and its footnote #2 for a practical acceptance of the Nuremberg Principle (denial of the Nuremberg Defense) and the associated but negative repercussions for doing so; and Chapter Three and its footnote #4 for a definition of intelligent subjectivity.

5. For more than fifteen years, most if not all crime laboratories have been very diligently testing all alleged cocaine cases for the illegal presence of cocaine and also for the presence of its nonaddictive and legal isomer (an isomer is a chemical substance that is structurally a "mirror image" of its twin). No thought is seriously entertained by crime laboratory management to discontinue this redundant testing because over these many years the nonaddictive isomer of cocaine has never been found *by itself* in a legitimate police case. Not having been found in a legitimate court case, there can be no confusion with the addictive form. The testing goes on and on for fears that the defense will raise the issue of this possible confusion at trial and the laboratory would then be embarrassed for "cutting short" the analysis and this would be most unprofessional to have done so! The logic in the situation is never addressed (that in thousands of tests the legal isomer has never been seen alone) nor is the fact that if the defense seriously contends that his one isolated case does contain the legal isomer, then the defense expert can try to demonstrate the singular presence of this isomer. No one has been able to do so yet. The prosecuting attorney has been placed in a position of constantly trying to prove a negative. This is deemed to be an excellent defense tactic "to muddy up the waters" in an effort to win an acquittal for his client, and most crime laboratories feed into this attempt by not taking a strong administrative position against it. A similar problem exists with LSD, and again the "experts" are chasing their tails for similar technical (criminalistic) reasons. As a society we have ceded the criminal justice system to these manipulators (tricksters) of the law and in doing so have accepted an inappropriate prosecutorial CYA philosophy that dilutes our more useful efforts in more difficult criminal cases.

Analogs are substituted synthetic (addicitive?) drugs (stimulants and depressants) that mimic the normal illegal drug, but because it has been deliberately and chemically changed and is then slightly different structurally from the illegal substance it itself is legal because it is technically a different substance. Due to the deliberate chemical manipulation, these substances are termed "designer drugs." The analog remains legal until the state legislatures catch up with the alteration and update the criminal statutes in this deliberate "cat-and-mouse" game. These cases, however, represent less than one percent of the total cases being submitted by the police to local crime laboratories. If one were to consider the activity given to these exceptions and the complicated and duplicated instrumentation justified and purchased to identify these substances, one would realize how disproportionate and unjustified such activity is to the normal case load and to the main goals of an understaffed crime laboratory.

As long as there are ample supplies of the "normal drug" on the illegal market the supply of these analogs (expensive and difficult to produce) will remain very low because the demand for them is "not out there." However, chemists being chemists and doing what chemists do best, the search goes on and is permitted to go on without any more meaningful alternatives allowed to be considered.

Another hair-splitting "witch hunt" of important note knowingly carried on by deceptive defense attorneys is the long controversy concerning the exact botanical identification of marijuana as *cannabis sativa L.* (Linnaeus), which can never be done. Any knowledgeable examiner knows that "linnaeus" is the designation of honor given to the name of the first person to identify and catalog a new specimen. This is a widely accepted practice in many scientific disciplines and has nothing to do with the technical identification of the actual specimen. Many defense attorneys have insisted that a false identification has been made unless the "Linnaeus" can be shown (included) in the identification. This is a deliberate manipulation of the written law and is an absolutely false interpretation of the statute that was tolerated by the courts for many years. No attorney would ever insist that the prosecution actually produce Miss Mapp or Mr. Escobedo when they cite and execute these rules of criminal law.

In other areas of similar interest, the withdrawal of a blood sample for blood-alcohol analysis and the subsequent positive report in a vehicular homicide case were denied admissibility in court when it was found that the nursing license of the experienced nurse who took the sample had "expired" the month before. The state law stated that only a "licensed" individual could take the blood sample. The defendant was released and all criminal charges were dismissed. The license was "reinstated" the next month when the late annual state fee was paid. No consideration was given to the fact that "a grace period" of weeks or months does exist in the same law, for any licensee to continue to practice a trade or drive a car, et cetera, and for the license to be fully reinstated with no suspension, disqualification or scorn and with full retroactive privileges. A hideous miscarriage of justice is obvious in all of these cases and in all too many more! This happens over and over again because there are too few proactive, energetic victim advocates in the criminal justice system.

6. Acceptance by these active learners of important but inappropriate professional values and belief systems are transmitted to the young and trusting analyst through making role models of their senior peers and supervisors. Truly, what we believe and accept, we "see" and then teach. Once the profession has been subverted it is all but impossible to correct the predicament from within the bureaucracy. In the vast majority, these individuals are paid at least 10 percent more salary while working in a crime laboratory than an ordinary chemist at the same level of experience working in a regular chemistry testing laboratory due to the fact that they have more difficult work to perform and are expected to shoulder more responsibilities than a "regular" chemist. If this extra effort is not rendered by these chemists in compliance with the expectations of the criminal justice system and the needs of the victims, juries, and the courts, then there is no need to maintain the higher salary or even a crime laboratory—the standard chemical testing laboratory would be more than sufficient. (See Chapter

Fourteen for elaboration on this very point.)

7. In the game of baseball this would be the equivalent of having a lifetime batting average of 1000 with nothing less being acceptable.

Chapter 7

THE UNBELIEVABLE SILENCE

The purpose of thinking is not to be right but to be effective. Being effective does eventually involve being right but there is a difference between the two. Being right means being right all the time; this demands an autocratic environment. Being effective means being right only at the end.

—De Bono

The shopping mall was a busy place with cars and people competing for space on this pleasant afternoon. It had rained for the last few days and everything looked and smelled so clean. A young woman is maneuvering her late model car over the speed bumps in this parking area, gradually edging her way onto the busy boulevard that will lead her to home. She had taken the afternoon off from work to do some badly needed shopping and to pick up a registered package at the post office. *These shopping malls were proving to be very convenient,* she said to herself. *Almost one-stop shopping and you can use the car as a safe depository for all the different bundles.* The hard part ahead, she mentally realized, was to get all these bundles into the apartment in one trip.

The area of the city in which she lived was set back several blocks from the shopping mall and bus transportation. The young woman enjoyed the advantages the area offered. It was a residential setting far enough away from the busy hub or central area. The apartment to which she was traveling was on the eighth floor of a high-rise that gave her family a nice view of the city, all of which she enjoyed—but at a distance.

Having found a parking space less than a block from her apartment, this businesswoman manipulated the various bundles in her arms while trying to locate her keys to the front door of the building. When the proper key was located, a second smaller key was deliberately linked to it. The family habit was that the first one to return home would pick up the mail in the vestibule alcove under the stairs. The balancing of the packages she was carrying while trying to retrieve the day's mail was an activity with which she was all too well familiar. Since she worked not far from the mall, she usually was the first home and had become adept at the maneuvers needed, as long as the packages weren't too big or heavy.

Determined as she was and fumbling with the mailbox cover, her attention was too concentrated to notice a young man quickly passing her on his way out of the building. For a moment this busy tenant thought she had experienced a dizzy spell because her view quickly became blurred in a swirl of moving walls, windows, a glimpse of the stairs and then the floor. She was glad she didn't need glasses, because they would have been broken in her fall. For some unknown reason she quickly became aware that her fall had not been due to a fainting spell, but that she had been knocked down, her purse taken, and the thief was now at the front door and moving fast. Disregarding the scattered bundles and a broken milk bottle that had spilled its contents on her, she sped after the cheating culprit, screaming as high as she could as she too exited the building.

The snatch was not as easy as others had been. This tenant was younger, fit, and a fighter. The scuffle had been as brief as it was one-sided because it was unexpected. *No one is going to take my purse and get away with it*, she vocalized to herself, *at least not without a fight*. The woman didn't realize until hours later that her head was badly bruised, her legs were in pain, as well as her feet, since she was now running after the thief in her stocking feet, her shoes lost in the middle of broken bags under the stairs. The thief was fast and out-distanced her within a half-block and upon turning into an alley, disappeared from sight. The loud commotion in the marble vestibule had attracted the attention of other ground-floor tenants, one of whom had called the police for assistance. Not realizing the service given to her by the unknown caller, the young woman was surprised, as she pondered her lost situation, to see a police car turn the corner as she retreated to her home, emptyhanded. Frantically waving the car down she explained her situation to the uniformed officers. Hours later it would be difficult to recall the unfamiliar, muddled details that happened so quickly. She did remember joining the officers in the car and the trio searching the neighborhood for a youth running from an unseen pursuer. The thief was not too hard to find when the experienced officers made several speed starts only to quickly stop at each corner or alleyway and look in both directions in this quiet neighborhood. Within one half hour of the assault, a youth fitting the general description was seen moving at a slow trot and quickly stopped when the police car came up behind him, having gained the advantage of going against traffic on this one way street. This was one effective method of escape, except against determined officers who had been detoured by these circumstances too often in the past.

At this mid-block stop, the young woman realized that her identification would be based upon the briefest glimpse that she had of the thief as he ran out the front door of the apartment and then only in view for a few seconds on the street. She was nervous, confused, and flustered at her predicament. In the excitement she did not realize until it was pointed out to her by one of the policemen that she held in her hand a patch of plaid cloth, seemingly a torn piece of cloth that matched to some degree the jacket the youth was wearing. The youth had a tear in his coat in the right pocket area. "How did it get in my hand?" she asked the officers. One officer replied that he "saw the cloth in her raised hand when he first saw her at curbside" as the police initially

91

responded to the call for assistance. A patch of colored plaid material appeared as one officer pried open the firmly clenched fist. "You must have pulled it from his coat as you fell from the assault back at the apartment," one officer replied. "We'll send the patch and this guy's coat to our crime laboratory and see if they can make a match," commented the second officer.

The young woman was escorted back to her apartment, after refusing medical aid, to pick up her packages and regain her composure after such an unexpected, busy afternoon.

The laboratory received the two pieces of evidence in due course with a copy of the police case report detailing the circumstances under which the evidence came into police custody. The subsequent laboratory report stated that "the two articles submitted for examination and comparison were similar in color, design, and construction but insufficient individualizing characteristics were present to make positive determination." It had been impossible to make a piece match of the patch to the plaid coat because a large portion of what had been a pocket was missing from the garment. Due to the lack of physical evidence the prosecutor's case was considerably weakened and the suspect was released since nothing in his possession could be linked to the assault. The purse and its contents were never found nor was the missing piece to the cloth pocket.

Was it truly impossible to respond to the needs of this victim or have we misplaced or otherwise lost the spirit of the criminalistic profession? By definition the profession is to interpret the physical sciences associated with a crime, to the criminal courts. In attempting to do so, were we allowing justice and common sense to be strangled by inappropriate professionalism is not giving more meaningful response to this type of evidence? Must every void in the evidence process be an irreconcilable difficulty that requires us to withhold the information from a jury? Certainly, there is no law that requires that such incomplete evidence be withheld from a jury whose obligation is to find the truth. (If the woman had torn a piece from the plaid coat pocket, would it have been unreasonable to assume, by extension, that the youth, seeing the damaged pocket, tore the remaining fragment from the coat and discarded it? Is this not a trusthworthy explanation of what most probably did actually happen?) Is not secondary circumstantial evidence (that which is something less than the very best) as potent as primary (a piece match of this torn patch to the pocket) evidence if it is believed to be reasonable by a jury? The unvarnished truth has to be in the affirmative! This evidence was of "the same color, design, and construction" as the defendant's coat and the opposite intact pocket. The plaid jacket had an outer pocket missing from the jacket. No mention was made by the laboratory of this subtheme. (Nor in the so many other cases; for example: human blood and hair specimens found in the toe area of the defendant's shoes that was different from his own but similar to the deceased, in a death by stomping; a small, marbled button found in a deserted car that was "missing" from a sweater worn by a homicide victim; a button in the hand of a rape victim with a similar button "missing" from the coat of the accused. Such presentations to the proper authorities is powerfully persuasive *but not final* until all the other "facts" in the case are in and the jury makes it decision as to the facts in the case.) There is a refusal to acknowledge that we must constantly deal with the unfortunate reality that most criminal cases are imperfect; that a realization of necessity binds these many intriguing coincidences, this heavy evidence, together. In not noticing this continuity, this disquiet reality, the coherent patterns, the comprehensive values,[1] were we being incredibly naive, impotent, and even an impediment to justice? Are we avoiding these series of latent, imperative connections because we wish to be isolated from any criticism regardless of the source or of the needs of the victims?

As court-recognized experts, can we not anticipate the reasonable features or plausible consequences in the evidence as any medical doctor anticipates the cause of a disease, its course, remedy, and degree of future patient rehabilitation? We all too often avoid these inner difficulties and tensions of not having developed the needed answers if the solutions fail to fit the image we have of ourselves as scientists. All too often we identify too closely with the problem's answer rather than identify with the problem if its answer is to be less than perfect. The only motivating factor to continue the struggle and not be satisfied with the easy (yes or no) answers is the instinctive feeling that we have a destiny beyond our past accomplishments and this drives us to these greater goals.

As court-recognized experts, we are exempt from the "hearsay rule" and may give our opinions to a jury in order to persuade them that our conclusions are reasonably true. The responsibilities of a professional criminalist are as different from a chemist as are the routines used. Our responsibilities in law are not intangible—they are all too real, sometimes flesh and blood. To meet these responsibilities to the victims (primary and secondary) we must be able to do more than the ordinary chemist; we should be able to take reasonable risks to make the incomplete evidence speak. What human endeavor is free of risk? Such risks must be handled in comparison to our abilities and to the need of the customers we are paid to serve. We have not been forced to accept our present positions; we are free to leave when or if the burdens become too heavy to bear even though the need remains as strong as ever. The partial solution is that we must take risks, but know our limits! We must acknowledge freely that we are capable of making mistakes—isn't that the very reason we gained experience, special qualifications, and training—to minimize that chance of error—but that must not prevent us from going up to these limits. We are dealing here with the collateral laws of necessity—of self-preservation, social justice, and public safety; these needs create in the responding agencies a higher obligation to perform then in most other professions! Aiding us to accomplish our professional goals as criminalists is the knowledge that what we see are not causal connections, credible coincidences, nor arbitrary choices. The items we notice are in response to the law of causality, cause and effect, and are trustworthy observations—that a thing cannot act in contradiction to its nature and therefore this trace evidence has significance and is worthy of jury consideration. We but need to find a way to measure and express this fact and unless we succeed we could very easily be found guilty of not assisting these victims of criminal violence through intellectual default. Such default permits the perpetrator to go free and the analyst becomes (at least morally) an accessory before the fact in the next crime committed by the released perpetrator, due to this negligence.

Since we apparently could not handle a simple comparison in this assault case, an absurdity in logic, we certainly cannot do so as the cases become more serious and demanding.

In another city, the normal and daily living activities absorb various individuals as they fill out their lives with meaningful personal and family errands. While doing so, for some reason, the normal citizen feels safer in the daylight hours than at night. For some reason we also feel safer in familiar areas than in strange, new, or different surroundings—perhaps because we have been there so often and nothing has happened to alert us of the dangers that can be so close.

The middle-aged woman had been shopping as usual in the neighborhood and returned to her safe apartment house and its familiar surroundings. After somehow picking up her mail in the lobby, the bags full of groceries hindered her from quickly opening the mailbox but she accomplished that feat as she had done so many times before. She then proceeded to the two-column elevator complex and pushed the up button for her sixth floor apartment. The apartment house was of the older type among many similar buildings in a neighborhood that had peaked but still was neat and clean and quiet and the elevators were slow. The mechanical devices of the one operating elevator responded slowly to the call from the first floor and started its descent. It was midday and the elevators had been idle for some time. The morning rush to work by her neighbors had gone. The heavily laden tenant did not know that the other elevator was stuck in the open position on the eighth floor.

As the elevator crept to the first floor, a male, situated on the third floor, noticed the elevator indicator moving down and as it passed the third floor in its descent, he pressed the up button. Mechanically, the elevator responded in exact sequence to both up demands for service. It stopped at the first floor for the single passenger with packages in hand and the front door apartment keys at the ready. This middle-aged widow had an unexpected destiny awaiting her as she pressed the up button for her sixth-floor home and the doors closed behind her. The elevator stopped at the third floor and upon opening two strangers met, and as he entered the cage to rob her of the few dollars remaining in her purse, he pressed the eighth-floor button.

Had the elevator opened at the third floor with two or more people in it nothing would have happened; had the elevator contained a single healthy male tenant nothing would have happened and the neighborhood would have continued to enjoy its serenity; but the elevator revealed an older woman, alone and with her arms full of packages. What could be better? A short struggle ensued. He only wanted her money. He had needs, too! He didn't mean to kill her but she would not give up that purse so he had to do what he had to do. The short elevator ride demanded forethought and quick action to insure his escape and he had come prepared to do whatever had to be done. He had prepared his escape route by having blocked the other elevator door with a wedge holding it on the eighth and top floor of the building prior to his appearance on the third floor. He would, after switching the block to the first elevator, use the waiting elevator to make his escape and go out as he had come in, quietly and unnoticed, with the unconscious victim isolated in the inoperative eighth floor carriage.

There is something loose in the air, something that guides circumstances, a product of causes that has no perversion to the end it is making, however contrary to our otherwise and most precise planning; some vital principle protests against the event, all actions or non-actions having consequences, most of which are unforeseen by anyone. A fortunate combination of circumstances develops that works against the spoiler and this cannot be denied. A connectivity that unleashes and forces blunders, positively correlated, gentle, unspoken connections, but insistent. In crisis, mistakes are made and wait to be found by any interested party. No one is totally in control of their fates no matter how good any of their plans might be.

As the elevator passed the third and the fourth floors, serendipity intervened. For some reason the elevator stopped between floors! Had he done something to prevent his own escape? Had she done something during the struggle that he had not seen? The reality was that he was alone in a four-by-four cage with a dead woman and the emergency bell was ringing and ringing and ringing.

On hearing the elevator bell, the middle-aged building manager went to the floor above the stalled elevator and with a key opened the outer doors to reveal the top of the elevator in a dark, deep hole. It was more than a foot below the upper level on which he was standing. In this instance he didn't need his brother who helped him take care of these buildings. It was a big job to clean the five-building complex, but the two of them did it, and for many years past. As brother number one descended to the roof of the stalled cage and opened the emergency elevator ceiling plate, a male, as if on springs, came out the top of the elevator, crawled over him and vaulted through the open, rear elevator doors. Brother number one looked into the elevator to see a tenant sprawled on the floor motionless. A mess to behold with the contents of the packages spilled about. How? Why? These were the mental questions asked and in response only silence was heard.

The woman was apparently dead, with a knife in her chest. Quickly regaining his composure and retracing his steps, the building manager ran to the front hallway window and looked out and down. He was in no position to give chase physically due to the distance and his poor reaction time to these unexpected circumstances. All he could do was see a young person running out the front door, taking three steps in a single vault, then running past brother number two! John, eight years younger, was there sweeping the sidewalk. "John—John," brother number one yelled, "stop that guy—he just killed Mrs. Johnson." Brother number two, unquestioning, dropped his broom and started to run after the young man who had just sprinted past him. The first runner was fast—he had a head start and he was young and the distance between the two of them increased.

Six blocks away a New York City police officer was on his post, near the more populated section in this bedroom community. (An elevated subway station was nearby, the mecca for the commuting public in the city. Those in the area had a cliché—"Where the subway comes up—rents went down." So true! This was not a wealthy neighborhood but there was a peaceful hue about it.) A voice was heard. "Stop him—stop him."

The officer could see a young man almost past him, being pursued by the caller. "Hold on there," shouted the officer as he went for his billy club. (On day tours, street patrolmen don't carry their nightsticks.) The young man was stopped; there was little he could have done against the uniformed officer. Brother number two, breathless, managed to blurt out that a killing had taken place in an apartment complex he and his brother managed. As the three retraced the distance they had just traveled, the officer stopped at a call box, gave the brief details as he knew them, and asked for assistance at the address given him. When they arrived at the apartment complex, police cars previously summoned were arriving. They quickly found and determined that the female tenant was dead. The elevator, with its unusual appearance, was lowered to the ground floor. A sequence of events went into effect as the information from the scene became known in wider and wider police circles. As would be expected under these circumstances, many "wheels" began turning on a broad field—each special unit being summoned to the scene was mindful of their responsibilities—the then prevailing priorities at each station and the knowledge that there was a sequence that had to be observed that slowed the investigation as these units did or didn't respond due to the distance to be traveled, manpower available at the time of notification, and high priority demands then in progress. From an outsider's point of view confusion reigned and a waste of manpower was obvious as police personnel moved about, waited, talked, laughed, and sometimes even worked at doing something.

The laboratory responded and started its processing of the elevator, but only after pictures were taken—laboratory technicians took the close-up shots, the photo unit taking the large, situational area shots. Each did so independently, but with coordination, and always before the medical examiner (M.E.) had made his investigation. When the M.E. had made his preliminary observations, the laboratory took possession of everything at the scene except the physical body. For reasons of decency, the clothes remained on the body only to be sent to the laboratory after autopsy along with, in this case, the small knife that remained in the body, as it was carefully covered and sent to the medical examiner's office.

The two brothers were questioned separately and their stories documented and signed. The young man suspected of the crime was kept out of the area entirely and was somewhere in the system being processed—photographed, questioned, fingerprinted, and questioned again and again by the responsible homicide detectives.

The laboratory continued its search for latent fingerprints, blood, and any other trace of evidence even to a cursory visit to the top of the elevator. There in the semidarkness a glove was found. It was obviously a man's dress glove—rather large and brown in color. It was placed in a plastic bag among other plastic bags of evidence containing the woman's personal property, the shopping bags she carried, the lifts of latent fingerprints found in the elevator car, and samples of her hair, for possible future comparisons.

In close questioning by the police investigators of brother number two, an interesting development happened. He had chased the young man some six blocks during which he had seen the suspect throw something into a street wastepaper basket along the way. He knew it was not the first or the last basket but one of the four or five that were located in this distance. As it turned out there were six baskets—one on each block. These baskets were quickly examined by uniformed police and in one basket a glove was found. It was sent to the laboratory in the normal course of events. Neither the laboratory or the police unit was aware that a second glove had been found until the evidence was assembled at the laboratory.

If one glove had been black and the other brown, if one was a woman's glove or a work glove, or if both gloves were right-or both left-handed they could never have been thought to have been a pair. However, there were no dissimilarities other than one being left and the other right handed. The pattern on the top and back matched as did the color and amount of wear to some extent. The fur inner lining could not be differentiated. The final laboratory report stated among many other specifics that "the gloves in question were similar to each other." The grand jury failed to indict due to the lack of firm identification.

Brother number one didn't see the suspect as he vaulted from the lighted elevator into the dark elevator shaft. Brother number one was night blind when the elevator episode occurred, having had the bright elevator lights temporarily blind him when he opened the hatch. Nothing was found (blood, prints, hair, or fibers) that placed the suspect at the scene! The gloves? It was stated that there could be at least five thousand pairs of the exact same gloves in the city at any given time with no means of differentiating them other than right from left. Brother number two didn't see a glove tossed into the basket. No one stood up to be counted. Not taking action minimizes the chances for making a mistake and, of course, everyone wants to do that![2]

A question comes to mind: Doesn't the victim have the same rights as our suspect? The victim of a criminal act is really the only one whose civil rights are not safeguarded. Even when they appeal to the defenders of the law they again suffer a violation of their rights. Once, when becoming a victim due to circumstances beyond their control and a second time, when they appeal for service from the system they supported and receive almost nothing, unless it is a sure thing (or more)! There seems to be too small, inappropriate, nonaggressive response to such a large opportunity on the part of those who should be, who are paid to be proactive professionals. There are hidden connections here that have high predictabilities that they are related. The collected evidence is not a casual, helter-skelter collection of just similar articles that have no lasting, mutual associations. The less than perfect evidence is comprehensible. It is absolutely wrong to be morally neutral under these circumstances. The evidence that can be found in so many crimes has the nucleus of truth in it and it must not be allowed to be stillborn. If the recipe given to us by Locard and Fleming contained any truth, the needs of the victims of criminal violence can be met by an authentic, sensitive criminalist. Therefore, we must not be like a stone lying in a riverbed for many years. When recovered and broken up, the stone is dry and brittle. Although surrounded by the water, the water has not penetrated it. Likewise, the victim's needs, our own ability, and compassion must overcome the existing dry technical voids that have prevented so many criminal cases from receiving legal review because we have become accustomed to enjoying too many cheap victories and that has ill-prepared us to seek the difficult solutions when more than the conventional methods are needed. We must not remain as unresponsive to our surroundings as that stone.

We are dealing with harsh reality and the fact of life that there are voids in the evidence. What the victims seemingly need is an interpreter of this reality who has the guts of their convictions and who is permitted to express these opinions in a court of law without administrative retaliation for trying or for failing, if an intelligent attempt is warranted. The creditability of this evidence and the reliability of the expert is a jury decision. If the incomplete evidence is not found or is found and is not persuasively presented the victims are violated twice. Isn't this prevention the very essence of criminalistics, its very dignity? There must be developed a means for risk assessment that expresses the realities of that which is less than visible or complete and allows us to reach beyond what we can see, touch, measure, and somehow develop the courage that expresses these convictions. We must challenge the injustice to these victims effectively with carefully made judgments, in logical progressions that are value orientations of our realistic expectations. Such cannot be automatic, instinctive, perfect,[3] involuntary, or infallible. If our motivations are to escape taking risks, a mechanism of absolutes that are not to be questioned is produced and if these clash with reality, reality is ignored! As professionals we cannot be conformists or allow the corporate selling of our souls. There is a moral imperative, a solemn obligation of conscience to be other than just safe and right. How can some of the best and brightest walk in such darkness for so long?

As experts for the criminal courts, we must have confidence in the system and not be technically sterile, ineffective, and out of touch with reality. We are called to witness, we are called to serve and to participate, and we are indigenous to the proper functioning of the system. In time of need, we must render more than "lip service" to the courts. The necessity to tell the truth cannot be held hostage to citing cases only that are absolute certain (or beyond) and within zero error parameters. We must reject the great myth of institutional infallibility and search for the court's directed reality in professional activism. The searching for just and necessary inferences, for reliable, cumulative, relevant evidence by knowledgeable, honest, ethical individuals can be successfully achieved by individuals with an open mind, honest heart, and a good conscience (a guide, a facilitator, a catalyst), when in contact with the God of their understanding (and as such) cannot err inordinately. We need a different quality of appraisal when faced with varying problems which will allow the needed extension of our observations to materialize. There are no guarantees and we fail the system if we hold fast solely to deductive logic, such singularity being viewed as a desperate attempt to generate soft answers rather than pattern matching. If we are to be true to the profession, the expert must be open to the use of deductive and inductive logic.[4] The latter sanctioning perception, interpretation experience, integration, corrective feedback and the ability to form sensible, logical conclusions from fragmented, biased facts in an effort to give illumination and clarification to the courts. It acknowledges a deterministic, orderly system in which tacit knowing is the affirmation of the possible, conveyed in qualified risk-taking statements, predictive influences, which is viewed as an obligation, not a choice. The fulfilling of this responsibility requires an inner eye, a mature, sensitive awareness that tries to see the evidence as if it were total, whole, and complete, not as an implication of chance, not a coincidence or disconnected circumstances but a recognition that these occurrences are unavoidably linked and are actually part of the inner order of things and can be expressed as a logical probability to a moral certainty, based on our experiences. It is realized that these victims of criminal violence have needs that are morally superior to the incomplete circumstances documenting most assaults. In any sense of justice they cannot be cast away due to a lack of courage or to an insufficient loyalty to conscience on the part of the examiner.

The authentic criminalist cannot be a passive interpreter of incomplete evidence; a cable must be thrown across the chasm that does exist in most criminal cases. Such an examiner is aware:

• That there exists a fundamental continuity between any crime (scene) and the source to the degree that consequences follow their antecedents with inexorable regularity (laws of gravity, of motion, and M-N-O-P events).[5] We should look at this reality cheerfully and optimistically as did Fleming and his predecessors;

• That in the incomplete evidence found, there is no perversity, no haphazard collection of possibilities, not random data nor any subterfuge;

• That the evidence does not lose its integrity because it is incomplete or indirect. Such items must at least be worthy of jury consideration as secondary circumstantial evidence;

• That such imperfect evidence need not be kept in isolation, unnoticed, unattended, unused, and untouchable because it is something less than the very best; that which is imperfect is not irrevelant in a holistic solution. The credibility of such exponentially increases as the number of such items and/or their points of comparison increase.

The authentic criminalist must translate the disquiet reality, found in so many criminal cases, by employing a new language of belief that presupposes:

• A mind that can compare, integrate, and relate to some reality [hidden unity] and with memory of the past, present, and with common horse sense, can anticipate the future.

• A reality where existence is *independent* of being encountered yet *yielding* substantial cognitive truth. [Example: the tree falling in the forest; a gestalt closure; an unexploded hand grenade.][6]

• An imperative of conscience [personal-ethical responsibility] to express a maximum value between the factual situation and the total range of the possible.

• High integrity of the analyst in considering the risk and degree of infusion of this convergency with truth.

• A search for meaning and wholeness totally dependent on an inner order; a subjective probability expressed as a realistic-access strategy is an act of faith in that order and is used as a measuring rod to the ideal truth. Such probability allows us to know more than the obvious.

• That the re-uniting of a pre-existing unity is the very apex of the criminalistic experience and any inappropriate denial is a paradox to the profession if such evidence is disowned in our efforts to elicit the truth.

• That the courts will accept exploring minds that are open to new patterns that cannot be limited to the mutually exclusive answers of "yes" or "no." The simple all or nothing policy answers or the sterile misuse of technology.

• That the courts will not be immobilized or be victims of the unknown, if it can be otherwise.

• That these criminal cases are too important to be decided by default, by limited vision, or by insensitive analysts whose loyalty to chemistry and its callous, fixed framework has become entrenched through isolation and who are morally inert to the needs of the victims of criminal violence.

• That there is no need for overwhelming test reinforcements (five tests are good—ten are better) on these biased evidence samples that are submitted by the police.[7]

• That we must make allowances for the impossibility of perfection in the vast majority of criminal evidence in recognition that the innocent majority have an inalienable right for adequate governmental protection against the villains in society (the toy gun syndrome).[8]

• That we are encouraged to take some initiative and not have the perceptions of a turtle. The extent that we do this is itself a moral yardstick of our fundamental decency.

• Finally we must be fully aware that as supervisors, managers, or as directors of crime laboratories, that what we have been taught and then believe as analysts—we have accepted and that which we have accepted—we "see" and then teach (only) that to others.[9]

MEANINGFUL DISCLOSURES

1. See the Preface and its footnote #1.

2. If truth really is our goal, it must be admitted that there was a possibility that the two gloves in question might never have been a pair—but under these circumstances it was a virtual impossibility, a high probability, that the correlation was correct; it was possible that the gloves had never been a pair *but* highly improbably that they had not been a pair; it was also *a jury decision* as to the reasonableness of fact in the matter.

3. The tendency to make mistakes is a chronic human condition that must be accepted. It took Thomas Edison more than a thousand tests on various substances before he finally discovered the properties of the incandescent bulb. When a peer criticized him concerning the number of tests, Edison replied that he now knew a thousand ways not to do it. If the truth were known, more has been accomplished by people making "mistakes" and learning by them than the world might like to admit. The only individuals who never make mistakes are liars or those who have accomplished very little in their lives.

4. In using *both* (rejecting neither) we avoid the folly of subjectivism, which imperfectly stated would be that when the objective standards now in force (in any discipline) are seen to be frequently violated and therefore are "imperfect," and being "imperfect," these standards must then be changed to reflect more correct and modern thought or methods.

The above is often held by many people to be true without realizing that to follow only subjectivism (the inductive route) is like a ship without a rudder, a home port, or a destination.

The deductive, objective standards need not be changed nor replaced when they often seem to be violated, but rather they are perfected when inductive reasoning is used in conjunction with them. The latter permits the shrewdly developed hidden agendas to be revealed. Inductive methods can go where deductive methods alone cannot, but only after the objective standards have been respected and with good reason to expand upon them. Used together, they are synergetic; used separately, one (deductive) is too limited to deal with corrupt hidden agendas that deliberately circumvent predetermined, known standards and the inductive route when used alone is too wild since it has no foundation from which to reasonably extrapolate. To recognize this false separation and to accept the reasonable consequences in joining them is an action to secure justice and human rights for the victims through the organized social response that is the criminal courts' and subsequent advocatory trial. This is the accepted arena where the hidden agendas are expected to be revealed.

5. We know the laws of nature as we know the letters of the alphabet. If we have the letters M, and N, and P, "we know" that the letter O is—has to be—the missing letter. This exact type of problem solving has allowed science to make many discoveries in astronomy, medicine, and physics. This "oddity" is strongly resisted and denied in present day criminalistics as it often has been over the centuries in other fields of endeavor. Most bureaucracies refuse to yield to any thoughts of change, from whatever

quarter, if such changes have the slightest aroma to threaten their cherished truths. The problems faced by Martin Luther (1483–1546) are no different then the problems of conscience faced by others, including Archbishop Raymond Hunthausen (Seattle) and Fathers Andrew Greeley (Chicago) and Charles Curran (Washington, D.C.), who are more modern victims to this intransigent, corporate attitude. See Chapter Fourteen and its footnotes #2 and #4 for a more recent continuance of this policy.

6. Can we not accurately deduce that if a tree freely falls in a forest and there is no human being there to hear it that it makes the exact same noise falling alone and unnoticed as it would if ten or a hundred people were there to testify to the tree's journey to the ground? The answer has to be a resounding *yes*!

If a person is given what appears to be a live hand grenade, must we pull the pin and watch the spoon fly off and the grenade explode in our face before "we know" that we have a live explosive in our possession?

We must develop a mental bridge that allows a legitimate leap in logic that acknowledges that the letter O, when found absent from the sequence, does follow M and N and precedes P; that the tree does not fall without making the exact noise just because we are not there to hear it; that the grenade will explode if we set the laws of physics in motion—because certain, reasonably expected occurrences will automatically follow. The principles of cause and effect are not accidental, unexpected, "natural" coincidences. Concerns of conscience expressing these truths must be vented and considered on their merits as established by the Nuremberg Principle.

7. In normal circumstances a case submission from a police action is a very biased piece of evidence against the perpetrator and where appropriate, in favor of the victim.

For example, when a narcotics case is submitted by the police to a crime laboratory the best filtering system imaginable has acknowledged its existence—the arrest process and the addict himself; his purchase and possession of the drug. He is an experienced street person, he knew exactly what he wanted and where to obtain it because he has been satisfied with the product many times in the past and he paid hard-earned money for the drug in this instance. Whenever possible, the drug should be tested but there is a limit to when the analyst begins "beating a dead horse," especially with an experienced evaluating analyst. In most cases the principles of qualitative organic chemistry (chemical derivatives) are severely violated when much redundant testing is thought to be justified and the operating laws of statistics ignored. Only if the analyst does not trust the police could this redundancy be appropriate, and then we have a much more serious problem that undermines all of society, police corruption. As criminalists our position *is not* to police the police. See Chapter Four and its footnote #6 for examination of the theory involved.

8. There must be developed a tolerance for the fact that mistakes will be made over any time period. This necessary allowance rejects administrative policies of CYA which places an inordinately high priority on professional self-preservation, even to the point of ignoring one's duty to society.

Memory recalls an incident when a uniformed police officer accidentally came upon "an armed robbery in progress" when he passed by a store while "on patrol" and noticed the raised palms of several people above a window display, through the store window. He realized that the customers had their hands raised in the air. He could not see the actual ongoing details then taking place in the store (due to the large window display) nor could he be seen from inside the store for the same reason. This officer had the option to race (in retreat?) to a distant telephone to request police assistance at this location. However, he realized that he, too, had a duty to perform and drew his weapon and entered the store; in that instant, he faced stark naked reality as only he could experience it. As the situation developed, many things quickly happened as he confronted and absorbed the scene. He was forced to shoot the perpetrator when the accused turned toward him with a gun in hand. The officer was later severely criticized for killing the perpetrator at the scene after it was discovered that the weapon used in the robbery was a "toy gun" which none of the five witnesses realized during the robbery. He was also accused by those who were quick to judge and not aware of the full story that "he had shot the perpetrator in the back in cold blood." This officer met his responsibilities to his chosen profession (duty) despite the well-known and predictable, after-the-fact difficulties he knew (somehow) would develop against him!

A subtheme to this same event was an unarmed, off-duty police officer who likewise came upon the same scene as it was being played out. He saw the uniformed police officer draw his weapon and enter the store, and the raised hands through the same display window moments later and did nothing to assist the uniformed officer in distress. This officer in civilian clothes was subjectively aware of the same information as the uniformed officer and had the same obligation (duty) to respond, but turned away and left the scene unnoticed. Days later, this individual boasted to the author that his philosophy of "no gun, no trouble" sure had paid off again. Not being armed when off duty (a violation of known, written department policy) prevented foolish actions and avoided the predictable criticisms of any actions he might otherwise have taken, from the public, press, and superiors in the "Monday morning aftershocks" that always followed such episodes. The fact that he deliberately ignored his responsibilities to a fellow officer known to be in need of support was never considered. He rationalized that his inactivity was necessary because he was, after all, unarmed. In this instance, two equally qualified persons saw the same set of circumstances and each was content to act opposite to the other. The off-duty officer, although he intentionally was unarmed, of course never left his police shield at home when off duty because then he would not be able to enjoy "free" transportation on the city's public transportation system!

This human situation is not at all unusual behavior since there are as many ways to take advantage of the system and still ignore our responsibilities to the system, as there are people in the system who wish to do so. The police action on the part of the uniformed officer had been a "good faith gesture" that absolutely must never be discouraged or discounted; otherwise, the second officer and his self-induced, dysfunctional philosophy will take hold by default and become pervasive in the (any) organization.

This episode has a direct parallelism to criminalistics when those who are encouraged and more than willing to follow a policy of CYA are rewarded and those who accept their professional responsibilities (reasonable professional risks) are put down (or worse) whenever there is any possibility of error in the cases they are handling. Two or more analysts can view the same evidence, and because somehow the evidence is incomplete have at least two different responses to make to the same event. Not to risk is always the safest method under all circumstances for personal and professional survival—except for the victims of criminal violence who have been dehumanized in the process and pay the price, in the street as well as in the laboratory. For criminalists not to accept and use inductive reasoning processes (arguments by reflection and professional common sense) and ethical considerations is identical to the off-duty police officer not carrying his weapon as required when he is off duty and in public areas. When the situation unexpectedly arises, but due to prior personal decisions not to get really involved, both fail to accept their chosen responsibilities and perform their associated duties. The fatal flaw is that secular humanism is alive and well and deeply rooted in most areas of our society. Since there is "no written law" requiring a more appropriate response, no effort is made (that which is not prohibited is permitted); therefore a medical doctor can pass by a serious accident scene and not stop to give assistance; an off-duty lifeguard can ignore the pleas of a swimmer in distress, et cetera.

Of course, the driver of a hit-and-run (leaving the scene of a accident) should never have done so, only because "it is against the law." Each of these individuals avoids the fact that there is a higher "law" that summons them (and in turn, all of us), although it is intangible and not written in any law book.

9. See Chapter Nine and its footnote #4.

Chapter 8

THE MEN IN BLUE

Absolute verification is a fiction never realized in practical science.
—R. Kelver

If your only tool is a hammer you begin to see everything in terms of nails.
—A. Maslow

The state of Washington is located in the northwest part of the United States and has to have some of the most picturesque settings of any part of the country, regardless of the seasons or time of day.

Situated between two beautifully visible mountain ranges running north and south and with the magnificent view of Mount Rainier directly to the south, the city of Seattle and its neighboring bedroom communities lie on either side of the equally beautiful Lake Washington. On a clear day all of these sights are within easy view of any commuter as he or she travels over the bridges and roadways in the greater Puget Sound area. The entire state of some 4 million people enjoys moderate weather year round, and is employed in a growing business environment due to the fact of being part of the Pacific rim. The state enjoys a relatively low crime rate with criminal activity concentrated in the largest city in the state, Seattle. The entire state has no more than five thousand sworn police officers and these are spread among 287 independent police agencies in thirty-nine counties. However, not all the population enjoys a busy but pleasant daylight commute to work in these pleasant surroundings. As in all other communities, emergency services are in place and actively doing their jobs regardless of the weather or time of day. The Washington State Patrol, which patrols the state's highways with its seven hundred officers, is no exception.

In the early morning hours in September 1974, on a lonely stretch of highway in the Mount Vernon area of Washington State, a locale just north of Seattle, a Washington state trooper can be seen talking to a motorist he has stopped for a speeding violation. He was as surprised to meet a young woman as the sole occupant of this speeding vehicle as she was to be stopped on this roadway at this early hour of a new day.

Both cars are parked on the extreme right shoulder of the road and due to the darkness both cars have their headlights on. The eerie blinking blue and red emergency lights of the state patrol car, parked to the rear and somewhat extended into the roadway,[1] spreads moving shadows on any reflecting surface. There is no other activity in the area to distract these two people in the necessary exchange of information that the officer requires, as he issues the summons.

Upon stopping her car, in response to the blinking emergency lights and siren of the patrol car, the sole occupant rolled down her car window and turned off her radio that had occupied her attention on her trip home. Through this open window, she handed her license and registration to the officer while his radio clearly chattered, periodically with a voice she could not understand. The entire necessary but unpleasant stop had taken about fifteen minutes of the woman's time, which was precious to her at this time of night and of small consequence to the officer because he was on duty. Unnoticed by either of these involved individuals is a pickup truck traveling the same road, but in the opposite direction. The nineteen-year-old male driver has just negotiated a sharp curve in the road and is less than one-half mile from the two parked cars on his extreme left side. The sole occupant of the pickup truck has been drinking and a later investigation will document that his blood alcohol is about .22 percent, well over the legal limit to be considered drunk while driving an automobile. In the eyes of a future investigator, the young driver has adjusted his forward travel to parallel the approaching traffic some distance away. The distance between the two locations closes rapidly. According to the civilian driver who just received the officer's summons for speeding, "There was, all of a sudden, blinding, bright lights and lots of noise and then nothing," she said when questioned about the serious accident that had just occurred, while she was sitting in the parked car and talking with the officer. "One minute the officer was there talking to me and the next minute he was gone." In less time than one heartbeat, a life was taken.

These circumstances, having occurred far north of Seattle and in the morning hours, required the primary investigative services of the local sheriff's department as well as those of the state patrol. This required many notifications by various radio dispatchers which started a chain of events, one of which was unseen by all participants, one that would extend far beyond this lonely stretch of road.

A telephone call was received some hours later at the small state patrol crime laboratory that was just then undergoing extensive staff consolidation. Three previously independent crime laboratories were beginning the initial steps towards administrative amalgamation, in response to a directive from Gov. Dan Evans, using a federal grant to increase technical staff services to all police agencies in the state of Washington, under the auspices of the state patrol. It was to be the first criminal case that the relatively new but experienced chief criminalist was to perform for the state patrol. He had been hired from the New York City crime laboratory as an individual with more than sixteen years of technical and administrative experience in crime laboratory work. The first six months (from April '74) had been spent coordinating the many details that such drastic changes required. It was to take a total of over eighteen months before the system was totally unified.

As soon as the laboratory opened its doors on this Wednesday morning, the chief criminalist became aware of the request to examine the scene of a hit-and-run death of an on-duty W.S.P. officer in Mount Vernon. By and large, the investigation took on the appearance of a textbook crime scene investigation. Upon arrival at the scene, numerous items of meaningful information concerning the collision of these three cars became evident. The offending pickup truck, showing severe damage to its left side, had been located by the police some distance away from the scene of this fatality with the operator still in the driver's seat.

The left sides of the civilian car and the protruding rear patrol car each received considerable damage to their entire lengths, for a distance of almost forty feet of metal. The single eyewitness stated that "The vehicle that hit us never stopped." If this statement is true, the vehicles were exposed to tremendous pressures to impart the structural damage that was so obvious to both cars. Numerous "piece matches" would be made of pieces of metal found at the scene. Cross transference of car point could be traced on all three cars as well as damage alignment, when the scene was reconstructed. The pickup truck had its front hood severely damaged, a deep dent three feet by two feet by six inches was measured and it was obvious that the driver had been forced to use the truck's window wipers to clear the windshield of the blood that was spread all over its surface.

Reconstruction of the accident confirmed that the offending vehicle had crossed the center roadway, sideswiped both cars for their entire lengths at a speed that would enable the truck to overcome the ever-increasing static resistance of the parked civilian car and the extended patrol car and then departed the scene, without stopping. The officer's body had been carried on the truck's hood and deposited on the shoulder of the roadway some seventy five feet behind the patrol car. It all happened in less time than it takes to tell it.

Upon returning to the laboratory that evening, the evidence gathered from the scene was processed in the normal manner. Several days later the officer's uniform and equipment were received at the laboratory and also examined. It was quickly noticed that the .357 magnum revolver, standard issue to all uniformed patrol officers, had its metal frame bent twenty degrees off the vertical at the butt end. Only a force of considerable magnitude against soft resilient flesh could have done that damage to such a formidable piece of metal. It was a virtual impossibility that this was an accidental coincidence, not reflecting the speed of the pickup truck at the time of impact.[2]

The subsequent report summarizing the circumstances and opinions of the chief criminalist concluded with a statement that "the offending vehicle had to be traveling at excessive speed at the time of impact." When issuing the report the writer knew that any defense attorney who would be hired to defend the accused in a future trial would "run him up one wall and down another" after reading that report. When asked, as "he knew" he would be by the prosecuting attorney some weeks after issuing the report, "What did you mean by the statement 'excessive speed' when the posted speed limit was thirty-five miles per hour in the area of the accident?" the investigator replied, "It is my opinion that the vehicle was traveling at least sixty miles per hour at the time of impact." The prosecutor quickly asked, "Will you state that opinion in open court, under oath, at trial?" The analyst answered, "Yes, I would," because there was compelling evidence to support that conclusion.

Many months later, in early 1975, the trial was held in Mount Vernon. Under normal circumstances the prosecution proceeds with the accusatory stage of the case first and is then followed by the defense and all its witnesses, if any. For some reason, the defense was permitted to place its expert witness (opposing the state's case) on the stand first, at the very beginning of the state's accusatory portion of the trial. This expert, with considerable experience in accident investigation, testified that there were no mechanical defects in the truck at the time of the accident and that in his opinion the offending vehicle was traveling "at a speed of less than thirty five miles per hour at the time of impact." A medical doctor then certified the death of the officer after the state resumed its proper sequence in the trial. The chief criminalist then took the stand for the prosecution and stated in turn his conclusion that "the truck had to be traveling in excess of sixty miles per hour at the point of impact." The defense, in its role, then began its cross examination of this stated opinion. The defense attorney soon established that the prosecution's expert was stating only his opinion; that the state's expert had not been at the scene at the time of the accident and that in reality the state's expert did not know exactly the speed of the truck when it hit the officer, all of which was true. (All of this was equally true of the defense expert but that fact was never stressed by the prosecution because it is a given whenever an expert gives his opinion that he was not at the scene when the accident occurred. It is also a given that the defense will, whenever possible, minimize the impact of any area of the prosecution's case.) The prosecutor then produced evidence from other experts that the driver had been operating his vehicle with a .22 percent blood alcohol level of intoxication, well over the legal limit of .15 percent.[3] The defense side of the case produced only character witnesses for the accused.

In due time the jury returned a guilty verdict but at a reduced level from the vehicle homicide charge pressed against the defendant originally. This was a severe disappointment to all concerned on the prosecution's side of the case. For weeks after the decision at any visit to the local police or prosecutor's office, where the topic was discussed, somewhere in the conversation a comment

118

was heard to the effect that "it was too bad about the reduced charge in such a case," that "if only. . . . "

It was an all too familiar phrase under similar circumstances, in so many cases in the past, too many cases. "If only . . . ." The little anxieties from so long ago, the growing uneasiness that the chief criminalist wanted to dismiss, returned.

The personal and perhaps biased attitude of the expert criminalist in this case was that the life of any police officer (or service man) is something very special. Together, they form two very thin lines of protection, locally and nationally, and because of their dedication to duty we all can sleep secure in peace and safety. It would be a brutal world without both. The W.S.P. officer had been killed in the line of duty at 3:00 A.M. while the rest of Washington slept.

The analyst felt a sense of obligation to pull all the stops in such cases; if not now, when? If not here, where? If not for him, who? His problem was that he had not really done anything more than what would have been done for anyone else because nothing more could have been done than what was done. Yet there remained a conflict that would not stay asleep. He felt uncomfortable and inauthentic. He questioned himself further by asking, *How could I have been more definite, more persuasive in my testimony? How could I have done more—if more was required to meet or exceed the jury's threshold of believabilty?"* [4] The total value of cumulative evidence and the incidental learning that he developed in other cases needed to be more meaningfully conveyed to the members of the jury and that was not done. He, as the chief criminalist, had faced this very problem so many times in the past and it was here again (the numerous, painful experiences of not being able to adequately cope with changing and imperfect case situations). It had been here before and he knew it would remain a problem and it would not go away. He cursed the impotency of his professional testimony because it seemed to be terribly wrong and this caused a crisis of conscience again. It had been like an itch that he could not scratch. Something deep inside him now snapped as this latent conflict surfaced again. There had to be something fundamentally and systematically wrong with a system that could not deal adequately with the realities present in so many cases. It was not that his professional belief system was insane but that it was totally inadequate to meet the needs of the victims of criminal violence. The irritation grew until the compulsion to act finally became irresistible. He came to realize that the profession was suffering from a disease of language that reflected a willful ignorance and an inability to confront the uncertain realities constantly present in many criminal cases. He had to somehow break down the barriers between these crime scenes and the jury's need to know! His long frustration in not having more impact on the jury's decision-making process as the expert for the prosecution had been like a time bomb for years ticking away until some inevitable day when he would be sufficiently induced to act. This was the day so long in coming. He had loved his science not wisely but too well. He had not been the enabler he was supposed to be. This was the precipitating incident that released previous inhibitions. He had been a guilty bystander once too often and it would not happen again. He realized that like so many other more direct, guilty bystanders, he too had ignored his conscience but was now given the opportunity to redeem himself and his profession if only an appropriate proactive system could be developed. The passive resistance, the discreet passivity that held him back from meeting his professional responsibilities, had to be overcome because the incomplete evidence in this and so many other criminal cases was so substantial and compelling, hauntingly relevant, far above what could be considered probable cause. It approached logical certainty that could not yet be expressed. Perhaps the many previous frustrations and failures had taught some compassion and sensitivity in the spirit of Jung's observation that "only the wounded doctor can heal."

To date, he had continued to follow the lead of his senior peers since he was in a subordinate position until he gradually obtained senior managerial rank and now shared a primary responsibility and leadership role in his profession and could start to translate his thoughts and desires into action. Almost immediately, he was faced with yet another very serious case and again had been unable to master the cirsumstances that faced him because he had not been given such a policy-making position to initiate change before in his career.

The chief criminalist considered the identified problem and realized that it was hard to speak of inner things, the internal tugs, and still harder to do this in a manner that could be understood by the general public when involved in difficult and diverse subjects. He knew there were common threads through all these past experiences but his professional training had not prepared him to deal more appropriately with this given realism—the disquiet evidence. (His pride in his chemical profession had been stronger than the desire to serve.) We were failing as witnesses for the prosecution to sufficiently acknowledge the existence of valid inferences and the collateral existence of logical expectations and predictabilities in the evidence that could explain the desirable accidents that almost constantly appeared. Was there hidden desire not to be confrontive even though we are the prosecutor's experts in this advocate system of justice? Was there a strong desire to maintain the status quo which helps to ignore any imperfections in the evidence and the associated professional risks, if these imperfections were to be expressed? Was it a method to avoid having to assume the responsibililty inherent in the criminalists profession?

He mused. Were we playing it safe, too safe; not fighting the good fight because we didn't want to get involved and were we violating a public trust in doing so? Was there a lack of courage preventing us from seeing the problem comprehensively and therefore not to seek new answers to problems that did not now exist?

How often had he been told "If it works—don't fix it"? It meant "Don't look" (don't improve on anything, don't look for or anticipate problems) because if you uncover a problem you will have to fix it and who wants or needs that additional headache and the resulting bureaucratic heat? Or was there something even more basic, a corporate wish to avoid any risks? (Do not place yourself in any position that will generate or receive any flak.) One thing he knew for certain—that for him to stay with the majority thinking while privately disliking it was hypocritical. He had to do something to quiet his conscience and correct the situation.

Hadn't he been given enough reasons to know that there was a real need out there? He knew that he was deeply hurt because of his professional conditioning as a chemist and he could not adequately respond to the need at this point in his long career. He and all other chemists had been both the beneficaries and servants of their own established system of analyses and that his had been disastrous for the victims of criminal violence. He knew that the problem he faced was no more intangible than the victims were abstract. His capacity for moral outrage overcame the cynicism he had experienced for too long. His professional responses to date had been pathetically inadequate and grotesquely out of balance to the need. He had to do something to quiet his conscience and correct the situation since he knew all too well that professional criminalists should not be judged on the number of their successes but on the keenness of their mental perceptions as demonstrated in their case reports and in their court testimonies and that this feature was almost totally lacking in his profession. To correct this situation he began a private research program to develop the necessary answers that seemed to be needed. It would be a conscious recognition of the interrelated, disquiet evidence that by insight he knew was there all the time. These mental anxieties gave him little peace. He now had a senior leadership position that required him, at last, to attempt to do what needed to be done. After years of finding fault and blaming others and privately complaining of their inadequacies, he now had reached a turning point in his career; this was his Rubicon.

It would take time and much effort and the cases kept coming in faster than he could solve the problems. It was at least a beginning toward the discovery of new currents in his profession.

MEANINGFUL DISCLOSURES

1. The police are instructed that when they stop any motorist for any reason, in addition to other safety measures, the patrol car is to be placed so as to have its left front fender area protrude into the roadway in order to protect the officer and the motorist if he steps out of his vehicle, from nearby oncoming traffic.

2. In criminal investigations of this type there have to be many individual subjective judgments made in order to make sense of the numerous and independent (detached and fragmented) artifacts found at such scenes. The investigator was not at the scene at the time of the occurrence but he must overcome this severe disadvantage and decipher the remnants inadvertently left there and attempt to come to some reasonable conclusions. These subjective inferences (expectations) will be his decisions recognizing the value inherent in the evidence. Admittedly, almost unlimited argumentative assumptions must be made and momentarily accepted if the case is to be solved. For example, that all three cars were relatively undamaged prior to the accident, especially on the sides of impact; that each of these vehicles being different makes, models, and years of manufacture, conformed relatively close to the manufacturers standard for that vehicle prior to the accident; that the blood found on the defendant's truck and front windshield was not there prior to the accident, and being the same blood type as the officer's known sample obtained at the

autopsy, belonged to the dead officer although science cannot and did not specifically confirm that the blood found on the truck belonged to the dead officer and to him only. It must be assumed that the weapon carried by the uniformed officer prior to the accident conformed in all respects to a normal service revolver issued to him by his department and that the damage to the weapon occurred as a result of a severe impact to the frame while the officer was wearing it in normal fashion and over which the officer had no control; that the officer followed normal police procedures in parking his patrol vehicle behind the civilian car. It must be further assumed that the witness, being a disinterested third party, is telling the truth of the matter to the best of her ability, barring a serious discrepancy with the accumulating evidence.

Further, that in order to meet the demands placed upon the investigator at each of the numerous scenes that he will encounter in his career, there can be no thought of coming to all the correct conclusions immediately, as if reading from some predetermined script. After viewing what has to be a confused, imperfect scene, scattered with incomplete pieces of broken evidence, all of the initial resolutions are inductive observations, subject to correction but based on the assumption that firm, natural, physical forces controlled the situation; then irresistible combinations gradually take shape in the analyst's mind deciphering and untangling the incident.

Each investigator has a duty to perform. It is a self-elected duty that was never forced upon him since this is his chosen profession. This duty becomes burdensome when seemingly unexplained and incontrovertible evidence opposing his view must be considered by the trial jury, for example, in this same case, the prosecution's medical expert testified that during the autopsy it was found that "there were no broken bones found in the officer's body." To this day this medical fact cannot be reconciled to the damage found at the scene of the accident. Regardless of the anticipated public ridicule (from the defense and certainly from others), the investigator, being conscience-bound, must give his opinion as to what he found and let the courts decide the actual facts in the matter. Only when his best efforts are adequately expressed to a jury can the investigator feel completed, regardless of their final decision. The Nuremberg Principle is intact!

See Chapter Eleven and its footnote #1 illustrating the further recognition of duty and value; see Chapter Four and its footnote #4 and Chapter Twelve and its footnote #1 for decision mechanisms.

3. Since the time of this accident, the level at which a person is considered to be driving while drunk has been lowered to .10 percent blood alcohol level.

4. See Chapter Twelve, Informative Reporting.

Chapter 9

A NEW ACCESS STRATEGY

The creative person can tolerate ambiguities and perplexities and is able to settle for probability rather than certainty. It involves adding something of one's own to the elements of experience making a new pattern which would not otherwise have come into being.

—I. Taylor

Laws are for men of ordinary understanding and should therefore be construed by the ordinary rules of common sense.

—Thomas Jefferson

There is a drum beating almost out of hearing. To experience its rhythm one needs only to sit alone, quietly, with one's thoughts, or some night try to sleep after being awakened by some small noise and you become aware of the sound in the distance. It's not exactly a drum, but a mind disturbance that is upsetting because it cannot be interpreted directly or totally. It doesn't get louder but it will not go away. It is the awakening of attitudes toward a more complete understanding; a concentration of alertness, an awakened awareness that begins to banish the unpalatable ignorance to which we have been exposed. There are feelings and thoughts of inadequacy to the many situations, the discernible patterns, that seem to elude us so often. We see the threads that lead us to a transparent barrier through which we cannot go, although there is a desire to do so that is strongly felt more at some times than at others. A silent nagging! A feeling that the truth is somehow being inadvertently suppressed by some inaction that is not obvious. It is a consciousness that the victims' needs are not being met. For some reason, some of the best evidence is not allowed to speak for itself. The opportunities do present themselves without hesitation almost in response to some great obedience that is unseen. The chance opportunities do become obvious and with these appearances comes a responsibility to somehow respond in a meaningful manner even though what we have is incomplete, less than the best. The willingness to support such evidence requires risk and wiser leadership, which in turn, in order to be effective, must produce results that are plausible, reasonable, persuasive, and consistent with a fundamental fairness to all concerned—society, the victims, and the accused. Somehow a new language must be developed that translates the unspoken, indisputable facts into a convincing presentation to a jury, reducing intellectual doubts as far as possible. There is a harmony existing in these automatic faith projections, these happy occurrences that must not remain unspoken. We must not let any misguided prudence hold us back; risk is as much an inseparable part of the interpretation as it is with life itself. Our written reports must be constructed in defense of what we see or of the truth that we believe exists. Evidence that is less than complete is not false, meaningless, weightless, or inadequate. We would severely limit ourselves if we were satisfied with only absolute truth; something considerably less must be sufficient because stark reality will not—cannot—produce such elevated demands. The victims of violent crimes who have been unjustifiably disgraced and hurt demand that we hear their needs and respond. We are too bound up with intellectual excuses, naive idealism and preconditioned responses, that avoid the real issues of establishing truth. We are presently too bound up with process, form, and service to self and less with substance and responsibility to the courts and to the victims. It is a fallacy that we can only deal with that which can be tested, measured, seen, or touched, never going beyond the safe academic mechanisms of technique. No value judgments are used here, just objective pigeonholes as if we were sorting the U.S. mail. Reason demands and therefore we know, we intuit, that a tree is falling in a forest does make the exact same noise even though there is no one there to hear it; the moon does have a backside to it; the sun is shining at night—in some other part of the world and even on an overcast day; there is order even in chaos.

We must devise a method that accepts the synthetic projections, the interpretative elements inconspicuously present in all experiences and test determinations. It must be a method that the prosecution can use to defend the rights of the victims before a jury that does not need indubitable conclusions in order to function. The court requirements do not demand such nor do the juries who must decide these cases. We as a society have breathed an ether that has dulled our senses and has almost put us to sleep if we believe that it is necessary to free nine guilty men rather than convict one innocent person. We must address each case independently with reasonableness and common sense so that the nine victims who have also appealed to the system for support and vindication are not left wanting. There is a great disregard of and disadvantage to these victims when the real truth is not spoken and given to a jury. We have set up artificial barriers against the expression of the truth by avoiding our own professional responsibilities. We have seen the enemy and it is us! We must develop a means of communication, of externalizing our internal technical obligations to the criminal courts and not be hesitant to do so. Without this wiser, reality-adjusted effort on our part, the victims of criminal violence will remain helpless, hopeless, and powerless! We must accept these possibilities when they present themselves because there is no one else to do it. We must not evade the demands of truth.

It is a mistaken notion to maintain that a crime laboratory

128

is only a fact finding, fact gathering, fact reporting unit. We are, through our reports and analyses, the accusers along with the prosecution in representing the victims in a court of criminal law. As experts for the criminal courts, chemists and the authentic criminalist are confronted with a professional contradiction. The chemist must admit that every scientific statement must, at best, be tentative; the criminalist, that each crime scene is an event-producing activity and the variations, the correlations, the at-one-ness seen by him can never reach a probability of one (that excludes all other possibilities). With the realization that a gap will always exist in both systems, the criminalist seeks to overcome the empty spaces while the chemist, marooned and neutral in the contest, stops, and because they are trapped by their own professional mechanisms, avoidance strategies and self-defeating conditioned response, he looks no farther. A closure of the gap[1] can be had but only after it is realized that it exists, that there is a serious need to fill it and if one is willing to take the risk, to do it. It is the acceptance that these relationships do exist, that of trust and of our own believableness. In such times of ultimate concern, inductive or intuitive probability can be the trigger functions for reality reformation that is an open-ended, a shared venture, with a believing jury. Our system of justice is not capable of problem solving without confrontation generated by a moral sensitivity to human values. The system must have a conscious intervention with experiences of value in response to our obligations and responsibilities. The basic decision is, do we hear the appeals in the evidence; do we see the intrinsic interdependence that does exist, the anticipated phenomenon, and take these value experiences seriously and respond to the obligation to make known the biased facts that are less than perfect and give a voice to these values that speak to our inner hearts? The probabilities that do exist in the facts and events must no longer be avoided; genuine reality must be given an opportunity to assert itself and not be restricted to professional preprogrammed perceptions.

It is understandable that professionally trained chemists do find it difficult to accept subjective probability since they limit themselves to a set of criteria that condemns as meaningless anything that cannot be verified by empirical inquiry. If this remains an impossible area for discussions due to their own elevated standards, then other areas such as moral life, love, death, taste, and art are also impossible to broach. This cannot be so—we cannot let it be so! The laboratory reports issued by a criminalist are not dispassionate narratives by eyewitnesses, but expert opinions that can use inductive probability statements, expressing the humility of the mind to accept and deal with the less than perfect situations. We cannot, as a profession, accept the systematic, culpable passivity, the shortsightedness, the loss of the moral imperatives that do exist in the evidence viewed. All too many reports to the courts lack these values that transcend the boundary of the analyst's self-interest. Chemists deal in prerequisites while a criminalist deals in the consequences of simple conviction, of the true, dependent, imperfect existences seen in the evidence that is inescapably compelling. A criminalist is a chemist with a conscience and this conscience is not being expressed on the many cases that fall short of practical certainty. The great majority of cases fall into an area less than certain but with initiative, skill and some risk to the analyst, these less than complete cases can be brought to the attention of the jury, if subjective probability is developed and utilized. The criminal courts do not require the expert to be absolutely certain before giving opinion testimony but that such testimony be rational, logical, and reasonable. The inherent credibililty of the disquiet realities so often seen in the incomplete evidence (the irresistible combinations) can be increased to a level of visibility, if the expert will use subjective probability and his own common sense.

The use of this inductive probability can be seen as a cauldron of opinion, a nonlinear precipitate of experiences, educated judgments, recollected images, with degrees of convictions expressed

· SCALE · OF · WEIGHTED · VALUES · OF · FORENSIC · SIGNIFICANCE ·

	(-1)	A (1)	B (2)	C (3)	D (4)	E (5)	F (6)	G (7)	H (8)	I (9)	J (10)
		>>> INCREASING			UNEQUIVOCAL		INDIVIDUALIZATION >>>				
EVIDENCE TYPES		INADEQUATE OR CONTAMINATED EVIDENCE / INCOMPATIBLE EVIDENCE OR REQUEST	SINGLE ITEM EVIDENCE SUBMISSIONS		GLASS, PAINT, OIL, DIRT & FIBER COMPARISONS / SALIVA, PLASTICS, GREASE, TAR, INK / FOOD STAINS / COSMETICS	HAIR SPECIMENS / SEMEN	SEROLOGY (ABO → ENZYME) / ARSON EVIDENCE	DOCUMENT EXAMINATIONS / GUN POWDER RESIDUES / MULTI LAYERED PAINT MATCH	TAGGED EXPLOSIVES (INTERNAL STANDARDS)	FINGERPRINTS / FIREARMS / TOOLMARKS / PIECE MATCHES / NARCOTIC IDENTIFICATION / BREATHALYZER / FOOT PRINT COMPARISONS	
WEIGHTED VALUES (VALUED JUDGEMENTS AS RESOLVED OPINIONS)	EVENT WAS POSSIBLE BUT IT DID NOT HAPPEN	NO PROBABLE VALUE	POSSIBLE		ONLY SUGGESTIVE PROBABILITY			PROBABILITY APPROACHING CERTAINTY		SCIENTIFIC OR PRACTICAL CERTAINTY / BEYOND A REASONABLE DOUBT	ABSOLUTE CERTAINTY *
DEGREES OF PROBABILITY (RESPONSIBLE EXTRAPOLATION OF EXPERIENCE)	ZERO	NOT SIGNIFICANT / INCONCLUSIVE MOST UNLIKELY / UNSUITABLE VERY LITTLE PROBABILITY			STRONG INDICATION / PROBABLE OF SOME SIGNIFICANCE / PLAUSIBLE & CREDIBLE		HIGHLY PROBABLE / VERY PROBABLE / HIGHLY SIGNIFICANT		MOST CERTAINLY (NOT) / MOST PROBABLY (NOT)	CERTITUDE * / ABSOLUTE IDENTIFICATION *	
FORENSIC CONFIDENCE LEVELS	ZERO	CLASS CHARACTERISTICS			SIGNIFICANT INDIVIDUAL CHARACTERISTICS + AND/OR EXPERTISE + SUBJECTIVE PROBABILITY				SIGNIFICANT INDIVIDUAL CHARACTERISTICS + CLASS CHARACTERISTICS } = DEGREES OF CERTITUDE		

* THE ONLY ITEMS CONSIDERED IN THIS CATEGORY IS DEATH AND THE FACT THAT NO ONE HAS ALL THE ANSWERS; WE WOULD LIKE OR NEED in incremental adjustments as controlled choices, not ingrained, rigid formalism nor ritualistic conformity to outdated maps of reality; it is a guarded cooperation with that which has been predictably uncoupled due to the circumstances involved. It is a fidelity to conscience to express assimilated case experiences and learning analyses to a court of law. As experts for the criminal courts, we must decipher the forest of facts, the hieroglyph that each criminal case represents, and reach a more comfortable plateau that expresses the complexities in each case. We must discover the reality—outwit the facts that cover, stifle, and keep secret this reality (evidence of things not seen) and reveal the truth. We must learn to be aware of and open to opportunistic circumstances whenever they occur. The use of analytical probability, serving as an incumbent, integrating function, helps us to articulate and give estimates of this reality at our risk because the expression of this reality is not a gift. If it is to be expressed, a price must be paid. Only an authentic criminalist, who has intellectual and moral concern, will understand this interdependency and the ethical imperative and will attempt to do what needs to be done. A professional criminalist fully realizes that he can never reach paradise, the satisfaction of all doubt. No amount of education, credentials, recommendations, apprenticeships, or experiences eliminates this risk. All such things are acquired for the specific purpose of reducing the probability of mishap but the beast refuses to go away. You can minimize it, you can tame it, but you cannot eliminate it. We must always be aware that the legal system does not require perfection or statements and opinions *ex-cathedra*, that a criminalist's first duty is to justice, not scientific purity and technique, that there is a personal responsibility for the results achieved ($+/-$), and for the realization of Locard's principles.

We abdicate our responsibilities to think when we acknowledge only those items reaching practical certainty (J). We must deal constructively with the art of the probability (always striving for inner certainty) with realistic judgment on the evidence that is cumulative, probative, and convergent. The law acknowledges that there can be no construct that explains it all, into which all the loose ends fit as if they were opposing saw blades before any firm answers will be given. The courts encourage their mentors never to feel too tired, weak, or frightened to struggle with the hard questions that have no preplanned, predictable set of responses; it realizes that the experts for the criminal courts must exercise arbitrary discretion in their reports in order to individualize the facts in each case. It realizes that accuracy is not the same as truth and that possibility of error must be endured as a learning process. The practice of criminalistics is an applied science[2], and it is a discipline that is never fully subject to logic or rule nor should it seek impossible guarantees; it is constructive problem solving and lays heavy emphasis on the individual, his flexibility and judgment and his responsibility to society through the courts. To do so requires more personal involvement in the decisions made with the knowledge that evidence that is considered reasonably possible (A–C) will not cut the mustard in a court of law but evidence that is reasonably probable (D) to that which is obviously certain (I–J) are all credible observations, merit indexes, worthy of jury consideration. With this understanding, as a rational intervention with the evidence, a meaningful curve shift can occur that is proactive and more interactive with the artifacts received from any crime scene. The reasonableness of these skilled opinions is the sum total of both our introspective experiences (intuitive inductions) and the credibility of the evidence examined, when expressed as a pluralism. This reaching (responsible, sensible extrapolations as guides to reality) gives meaning, worth, and significance to the evidence by harmonizing, integrating, and coordinating the ideal potentialities in the evidence in light of our integrated, reconstructed experiences. To the degree that these observations are necessary and sufficient, inductive probability is the living, positive response of the believer. We must risk our necks upon the probability that the same regularities, the substantial similarities and discernible patterns observed in the past will indisputably continue in the future. This believing arises in us as an inner personal conviction to the situation, events, objects, relations and symbols which we recognize as expressions of the truth, which we understand and then speak. This response is an emerging pattern, whose main lines not only fit but extend what we have understood before. Through this progressive, internalized process of thought, we allow old truths to grow by new truth additions (expansion and assimilation).

Once a significant credibility threshold has been reached (an imperative expectation, and active, optimistic belief of things not seen), the emphatic probability of the situation, a confidence titer, or degrees of reliability, increases disproportionately to the right, and we then have built quality bridges, using constructive dialogue, across the inevitable technical voids, more effectively addressing the evidence in each case. We have reached the action level of commitment! We have filled the gap! A better gestalt is formed! This requires courage, honesty, and initiative and audacious self-confidence in the (infallible) belief of the intrinsic interdependence of eternal recurrence and of order (cause and effect). This strategy offers high flexibility—a higher ratio of solutions to problems. The bench mark for jury consideration, the lace curtain, the veil, has been responsibly raised; the no-fault thinking has been curtailed to society's benefit. The common judgment of good people (the jury) can now be made. This desire for reasonableness renounces the previously mentioned extremisms as frauds. The real, more experienced expert, as a processor of grim reality has taken his rightful place in our adversary system of justice by not limiting his testimony to unequivocal report writing, but by mixing, by integrating his acquired convictions, his anticipations, and his knowledge, with pervasive caring.

If the foregoing has any merit, the effect should be a dizzying reversal of the thought patterns not unlike the Copernicus effect in astronomy.[3] It is the duty of sincere court experts to produce a confrontation with reality, through their written reports, that unveils both unvarnished facts in criminal cases and the vital reality that exists, void of timidity and not antithetical to the natural law. The role of law provides proportionate and meaningful responses to various violations of norms and for criminalists to do less imperils reality, common sense, and good judgment. The very best that can be obtained is to continually try to be wise in our judgments, sober and honest in all appraisals, giving calibrated opinions that allow us to more appropriately respond to these human tragedies. These necessary pluralisms, to deal with the multiplicity of facts and explanations are to be attached to each case in an ad hoc fashion. The salt of justice would be bland if we were to do otherwise. We must be comprehensively involved. The courts do allow realistic goals to be obtained—not the all or nothing decisions (mindless obedience). Realistically, there are no guided tours in criminal cases (scenes), only an imperfect mosaic of events, interlocking relationships always present, waiting to be found. To accept the foregoing, experts must accept a shift in their approach to their case analyses because the use of internalized, analytical probability prohibits inaction, paralysis, and shrinking violets. There must be a mental evolution from behaving like a person struggling to professionally survive (positive selfishness) to behaving like a concerned expert, choosing to evolve. We must resolve our technical environments through a change in our priorities and accept the associated responsibilities (issues of conscience) that cannot be delegated to others and that are implicit to the role of an authentic criminalist. We must give up the idea of only doing casework that we can do perfectly and of being experts only in the noncontroversial and the negative cohesiveness existing in the profession. Criminalists must have sincerity and courage or perish! By our extreme passivity we deny effective assistance to law enforcement agencies, to the courts, and to the victims of criminal violence. Heretofore, we have correctly assumed that the burden of proof in a criminal case is for the prosecutor to establish the guilt beyond a reasonable doubt and therefore, the criminal justice system has the right to expect the authentic expert witness to testify even when we cannot tell the whole truth; we must tell the truth as we know it to be. We must penetrate material reality. We reject the conventional wisdom that it is better to risk loss of truth than chance any error. The jury has the right to hear all the evidence before they make their decisions. The victims deserve their day in court!

Since such narrow viewpoints as zero error and absolute certainty, mistakenly conceived as conservatism, are entrenched in the profession, there will be relatively fewer reports ultimately submitted to court for jury consideration and fewer judgmental decisions will be open to the jurors, thus manipulating the guardians of the system, if not the system itself since the jury's decision making capacity is undermined in advance. Justice that is delayed or curtailed is justice denied. It was never intended that any criminalist was ever to be placed in such a final decision-making position because we are not surrogate jurors. As analysts for the prosecution, we have an obligation to render informative reports from the analysis of crime scene evidence. From the lack of meaningful reports, it would appear that many practitioners in criminalistics have no enthusiasm for, and have failed to grasp the spirit and essence of our advocate system of justice, progress by conflict within the law. During each of these detailed analyses, the expert's mind, eyes, perception, learned abilities, and memory are concentrated on the exemplars submitted for comparison. His judgment is an accumulation of bytes, each thread altering his reflective mind balance in one direction or another until, fragment by fragment, rationally credible, a weighted decision can be made. During this inner dialogue, there is much vacillation, rejection, evaluations, selections, associations, erasures, reflections, interpolations, coupled with being encountered with the objective world.

As he approaches certainty, cumulative individualizations of forensic significance, intuitive seeing of necessary relations that become apparent to him, are sane, sensible correlations that are worthy of belief. The transfer of these subjective, expert observations (value classifications) to a jury of his peers, must be expressed in as forceful a manner as possible, fully reflecting the analyst's detached, weighted data collections in degrees of subjective probabilities (predictive indexes, subjective predictions, or belief responses) C.H. These are thoughts, inquistive reflections, insights, degrees of belief and reasonable expectations of the truth made flesh. Such decisions are a burden to the jury, but that specifically is their assignment and responsibiltiy as they express the community's conscience to resolve these doubts on issues of fact. The jury is entitled to see that evidence and to hear the expert's explanation, rational reconstruction, and evaluation of it. To be impartial, intellectually responsible professional criminalists have no other alternative but to meaningfully articulate their observations and perceptions to the courts. We must not only desire the truth, but we must live it and give it meaning. We come to the conclusion that a sensitive criminalist cannot avoid making decisions less than certainty if the evidence cannot support a higher level of belief. It is an effort and is of much value to push rational inquiry as far as it will go to bridge, with constructive dialogue, the chasm between submitted, imperfect evidence and the jury's need to know. This expertise must be meaningfully applied to the pragmatic needs of criminalistics using nuanced statements expressing choice under risk. This is the indispensable duty that the true professional criminalist must meet.

FEDERAL SUPPORT

There have been many other concerned individuals, especially on the federal level, who have seen a need to improve crime laboratory performance in general and increase the professionalism of the nation's law enforcement community in particular. In 1968, President Lyndon B. Johnson signed into law a federal aid bill which established the Law Enforcement Assistance Administration (LEAA). A small portion of this bill required each of the fifty states to create their own crime laboratories and then cease to send the preponderance of their criminal cases to the FBI laboratory in Washington, D.C. This federal laboratory was becoming swamped with far too many cases from all over the nation and it would not be able to handle the anticipated and growing case load from the states.

Within a few years the profession of criminalistics was forced to greatly expand. From a nucleus of about twenty-five-plus crime laboratories existing prior to the bill, the nation built over two-hundred plus additional crime laboratories and all of these required technical staffs for them to function. The solution to the problems documented in the bill (money) arrived with such speed that the nation's universities could not meet the demand to educate professional criminalists (chemists versed in scientific jurisprudence) and the need was critical nationwide. A mismatch gradually occurred because the new crime laboratories that were created almost out of thin air were to be staffed by professional chemists not criminalists. These professionals who filled this vacuum were to have no police training, no meaningful exposure to even minor crime scenes, and brought with them the passive professional attitudes of a consummate chemist. These professionals acknowledge only literal truth and the objective aspects in any criminal (evidence) case and thereby become subjectively detached from the victims they are to serve. Consequently, because there was little clinical training (exposure to practical reality) mixed with poor managerial direction and few meaningful promotions, there developed little bonding between these professional chemists and the victims of criminal violence. The needed confluence of conscience (moral reasoning) and expertise was thwarted by this disengagement, a wrongful bureaucratic interpretation and application of the law then followed and became entrenched. An inappropriate, chronic, artificial selection process gradually took hold of this newest profession.

Since criminalists could not be produced in sufficient numbers, the chemists who were originally employed under this federal professionalization program were in time promoted to managerial positions and other chemists were hired to replace them, none of whom were to accept the proactive role required of a criminalist in a court of law. This fatal flaw deluded the criminalistic profession and placed in positions of influence experts without a shared or personal responsibilty with the victim; this insulated these experts from the realities of the real world and is the core cause for the failure of present day criminalistics to meaningfully respond to the victim's needs. There was no pause to analyze or later evaluate the problems that were created by this federal intervention. The professional chemists were academically educated by fact acquisition and memorization methods—not trained by problem solving learning.[4] This produced qualified chemists but not good techical investiagators. It produced experts who possessed conflicting purposes that are for the most part extremely limited, too focused, and irreconcilable to the needs of the criminal justice system. The profession of criminalistics became preempted by professional chemists (herd effect) with all their endemic, inappropriate authoritarian baggage. This includes their homogeneity of thought and process that denies the existence of a long continuity of predictable precursors in the real world situations they encounter in so many criminal cases. As a direct result of this artificial mutation of personnel, the supply and demand urgency at the university level to produce professional criminalists (seed corn) quickly became shunted. The previously heavy police-victim orientation quickly changed to almost complete national civilianization of the group which then materially helped protect the now entrenched usurpers of this fledgling profession. Since personnel hiring policies do reflect future work policy, an entirely inappropriate philosophy took root even to the point that those in leadership positions took comfort and support when years later a distinquished peer stated in a professional journal (April 1975) the current philosophy: "The criminalistics community should abandon its attempt to effect a bonding between law and science and the effort instead be diverted toward an enhancement of technical correctness."

The needs of the chemical profession were therefore to take a superior position to the needs of the criminal courts, of law enforcement, and of the victims in a very self-serving, risk-free,[5] professional environment. There is nothing wrong with this development, if it were in any other profession but criminalistics. It is a well-established fact that the preponderance of individuals respond to and are a product of the environment in which they find themselves; but the strong internal dynamics of the chemical profession for this technical correctness in criminalistics is hurtful and warped ideology producing unsuitable and flawed intangibles for those who wish to become authentic criminalists and for the victims of criminal violence.[6] Over the years, no challenge to this conventional scientific perspective was to be heard among professional criminalists; there was to be no allowance in case analyses for the inevitability or, rather, the probability, of working with imperfect cases. The inability to encourage insightful proactive examinations on the various criminal cases became lethal ignorance for law enforcement, for the victims, their families, and for the criminal courts. The needs of the victims and the interests of the professional chemist are obviously not identical, since the latter is so cold, calculating, and detached, whereas these victims' needs are identical to the interests of an authentic criminalist who is aware that the need for victim advocacy transcends the normal rules when one is working in an advocatory system of justice and it is he who has the will to do so, if possible. It is he who can meaningfully respond to the basic

140

issue that constantly recurs in all these criminal investigations, namely, "What is the essential reality of the situation?"

There are over 5.5 million victims of criminal violence each year in the U.S., and forty-nine out of each fifty of these cases never obtain a conviction because the vast majority of these cases are never submitted to court for trial. Under these conditions, the down-to-earth reality that no single case can legitimately be submitted to a court of law without being couched in some terms of subjective, predictive, analytical probability is avoided. Only cases reaching zero error and proven beyond a scientific doubt are submitted to these courts of law; any other evidence or information developed that is less than perfect is virtually stillborn. However, in reality all crime laboratory reports do require statements of subjective probability if the real truth were known and accepted. Such reporting methods using subjective, expert probability must be adopted not so much from free choice as from a technical and moral necessity. Anyone who is at all in touch with the reality as it exists today in the criminal justice system (CJS) will be, has to be, fundamentally dissatisfied with the way things are (50:1) and have been for these many years. The unanticipated possibilities in so many thousands of criminal cases must not remain silent and lost due to our lack of courage, our being blind to what is all too apparent or to our inability to articulate the harmonies and continuities in nature that are now lost to the mechanics of chemical technique and analytical finesse. A realignment of our professional goals is desperately needed to deal with this dysfunctionalism, seen as a flagrant miscarriage of justice, in the nation's crime laboratories.

A case comes to mind that surely reflects our obligation to speak out—the silent necessity could not be louder, more piercing or more obvious and has a direct bearing in all that has been mentioned so far in these pages.

Of all the criminal cases coming into a crime laboratory, none was more pathetic than that of Ms. Kitty Genovese, who died an early and unnecessary death in March 1964. This case was to have a lasting effect on this writer.

This victim of criminal violence was a twenty-eight-year-old woman with dark, straight hair combed over a very fragile body. She was returning to her home located in a densely residential area, from her place of employment at about 3:00 A.M. one morning. As was her usual practice, one that many neighbors shared, she parked her car at the now empty railroad station parking lot more than a city block from her home. Proceeding to her apartment in this middle class, crowded metropolitan area, the young woman was seriously assaulted by a male who struck from the shadows on this deserted city street. She was stabbed repeatedly but not yet fatally. For more than forty minutes she screamed for help to her sleeping neighbors of who, thirty-five, recalling the incident the next day, ignored her pleas. They too realized all too well that, by tradition, they should not get themselves involved for fear of having her misery somehow transferred, shifted to themselves. "It is not our problem," they uttered to themselves in a weak self-defense posture. "Smart people don't ever get involved" was (and still is) a well known cliché even to the point that only one person eventually made a phone call to the police—fifty minutes too late.

After the initial attack, the young woman crawled some two hundred feet to seek shelter from the terrible night, only to be traced to her point of concealment by the returning perpetrator. He had initially fled from the area when apartment lights were turned on and shouts to Ms. Genovese to "be quiet" and "go someplace else" were heard. When these lights finally went out and the neighborhood was again quiet, the killer returned and sought out his victim in a secluded apartment vestibule that she had reached in hope, but in vain. Kitty Genovese was then assaulted again and this time died in this hallway. No one came to her aid in this hour of desperate need. There was an absolute demand for someone to come to her aid and it was denied. No one spoke for her now nor in the days to come.

142

On hearing of the case a day later, unpacking the evidence at the crime laboratory, you wished to be of some service. Where had serendipity gone in this case? Where was it now hiding? What was present and so obvious but not yet seen? What pair of glasses could be worn to see the ishihara-like pattern[7] that most probably was there?

In this case, during the crime scene search, a piece of clothing was noticed to be missing for no apparent reason. Weeks later, through police investigation, questioning, and subsequent search, a suspect was identified and the article of missing apparel found with a red stain on it, similar to her vital fluids. Was this a pattern like so many other cases, yet, different in many respects from all the others? What unseen, unnamed source taunts us? No laboratory report was to identify this human blood stain to be that of Kitty Genovese.[8] The rhetorically weak, opaque report symbolically reflected the subjective indifference, the almost carefree, the strict objectivity of the trained methodical analyst.[9]

There is no law to punish the cruel, vulgar people, the uncaring neighbors of Kitty Genovese, the unseen but deaf listeners. Nor is there case law against those experts who see the evidence in such cases but in a self-defensive mode refuse to make any reference to it and the consequences of their subsequent nonaction(s) are never envisioned. The pain suffered by the victims of criminal violence should not remain solely to themselves. Their pain and subsequent need for an appropriate response is as great as was that of Kitty Genovese, on that lonely street in Queens, New York, so long ago. If their need remains severe and our professional, analytical bench marks for decision making remain equally high, our subsequent, subjective inactivity will not adequately redress the wrongs committed. If any soldier did as little, if any police officer, lifeguard, astronaut, test pilot, fireman, doctor, bridge builder, acrobat, racing car driver, or coal miner became so detached and impersonal from the concerns, from the risks and the consequences of their chosen professions, they would cease to exist as a meaningful participant in that profession. Are we criminalists any less guilty because the implications of our silence is as staggering (for the victims of criminal violence) as the silence on that deserted street in Queens when we insist on the absolutes as demanded in Arizona; when we reject the inductive regularities, the known predictabilities, the anticipatory information and refuse to use analytical probability, reasonably? We cannot accept or permit these other professionals (police, astronaut, servicemen, et cetera) to put aside their inherent professional responsibilities when prudence would indicate that they hold back. No war was ever won if the professionals who fought it insisted on keeping their heads below the parapets. Nor can we now allow ourselves this luxury to avoid these professional risks if we are to meet our own significant personal/professional obligations. To do either would be reprehensible, a hypocritical double standard for us all. Such risk comes with the territory in each of these instances. The controversial policy of "zero error" and "beyond a scientific doubt" are professionally self-serving and irresponsible methods to maintain invulnerability; under this scheme there will be no enthusiasm to consider the workability of an extrapolation curve which would give more meaning to the incomplete (detached) items of evidence so often found in criminal cases. The professional chemist has been allowed to become too isolated to be as effective as he otherwise might be. He has become like an old lion—old and ragged without teeth and without claws, waiting upon others for its food. To a large extent, the professional chemist allows himself to be controlled by professional dictates because he wants to be controlled using these high standards as a shield so he can be professionally safe and risk-free. He has learned, by example, that the only way to succeed is to never make a mistake and to do a minimal job in interpreting the evidence before him. However, these professional chemists are not employed in crime laboratories for their own careerism, to protect these professional standards, or to hide behind them. It is estimated that a professional chemist working in criminalistics is much like a pacifist working for Dow Chemical Company in a munitions plant. Both are competent but certainly not innovators and both are disloyal to the efficient generation of the needed products.

We must somehow overcome the above difficulties, become professionally tolerant of the less than perfect cases, and become much more effective in a court of criminal law by adequately addressing the multiple of variables always present in criminal cases. Such professionals must possess a fearless fear that articulates the realistic expectations of a penetrating observer. As professional experts for the criminal courts we must be aware of the detached harmony, the at-one-ness that does exist in so many cases and express this as a probability; that these voids in the incomplete evidence are not separate but were joined. Criminalistics is a very need-satisfying profession and requires sensitive, creative thinking behavior in order to use inductive probability.

A more earthy statement addressing the exact point is: "A ship is secure from the perils of a storm in a safe harbor—but the ship is not built to always remain in a safe harbor during a storm."

MEANINGFUL DISCLOSURES

1. See Chapter Four and its footnote #4

2. It is fundamental chemistry with the professional excesses (misplaced priorities) removed. Therefore, a criminalist is a pragmatist who is professionally immersed in life's messier realities and who is always haunted by the ideal to have all the pieces to each puzzle, being able to prove all cases beyond a scientific doubt while maintaining zero error in all analyses. If this extreme desire is ever alluded to by the courts, justice would be impossible to be obtained and no sensible person would even try to comply.

3. Copernicus (1473–1543) was a Polish astronomer who

postulated that the sun in the universe actually stood still and the other planets, including the earth, rotated around it. For the previous fourteen hundred centuries the "scientific community" thought the exact reverse was true. After all, using deductive-objective reasoning, one could stand still in one place and during the day "see" the sun move from the east in the morning to overhead at midday and set in the west in the evening. Didn't such objective observations prove that the world stood still and the sun moved? It took the scientific community another 150 years to reverse their thinking, denounce the objective method, and accept the Copernicus theory.

In a similar fashion, Dr. I. Semmelweiss (1818–1865), a Hungarian physician, pioneered antisepsis in obstetrics, which completely upset the medical establishment's cherished but incorrect theories. Dr. Semmelweiss noticed (inductively) that "there was some kind of a connection" between the deaths of many pregnant women when young physicians performed autopsies and then went to another area of the hospital and examined women in childbirth. Dr Semmelweiss did not know the specifics of the affliction but subjectively he became aware of a concealed pattern that had to be penetrated and through trial and error, he symptomatically bridged the gap in his professional knowledge and deciphered the problem. He strongly recommended that the medical personnel wash their hands in chlorinated water upon entering the obstetrics ward. He demonstrated that when this was done, there was a drastic drop in the death rates of these women in the ward. Many hundreds of woman were to continue to die needless deaths from puerperal fever before the new theory concerning infections was accepted only after fierce medical opposition. There was nothing obviously wrong with the cherished objective methods then in practice because the (then) unknown bacteria killing these women could not be seen, tasted, measured, or smelled or otherwise identified—but it was there and the female patients "paid the price" for this continued professional oversight.

146

Compassion for these victims was the major element that separated Dr. Semmelweiss from his knowledgeable peers and their rejection of him. Having this one additonal element permitted this expert to venture into the unknown and deal with the same unknown that his peers rejected as being absurd. (Again, at least two groups "saw" the same set of circumstances and were content to take the opposite track. The "medical authorities" were ignoring their duty to their patients due to an inflexible mind set egotistically maintained for another fifteen more years after the profile was described to them!)

4. For generations, there has been an academic war between university, academically educated professionals and those who are of the opinion that such education should have practical aspects to it. The pure academics are steeped in the theoretical, research oriented, non-pragmatic approach to problem solving, learning for the sake of learning and of gaining pure knowledge for its own sake. It is at these academic institutions that the rules for the corporate arena have been written without any regard for factual reality. Since it is entirely a creature of "the academy" no primary consideration is given at the university level to apply this acquired knowledge to solve normal, everyday problems in the workplace of any particular profession. In the elevated academic strata (ivory tower), there is great disdain for and, consequently, little consideration given to solving problems through the applied sciences "where the tire meets the roadway," the practical application of the acquired body of knowledge. At the college level you are educated (in the school of John Ruskin-Newman and John Mills) and never trained (as per Herbert Spencer). This approach and its ingrained, elevated attitude is implanted at the university and carried unquestionably forward into the workplace by these professional graduates as a mind set, to the detriment of the victims of criminal violence, when these "experts" must deal with harsh reality and an untidy, fragmented world. Little consideration is given to the fact that the philosophy

taught and accepted is static and programmed with little motivation to change. In the modern age of space exploration, high tech megabyte computers and artificial intelligence, the elitist approach to general education is passe. These academics are not preparing their students to meet the real world. Ethics and moral duty are, of course, almost never taught to these "science" students and in the absence of such instructions, only self-serving secular humanism is left to fill the created void.

5. See Preface and its footnote #1 for more detailed information.

6. To always be objective sounds plausible by any open-minded standard, except to anyone with a modicum of understanding of human nature. Such awareness demands the constant use of inductive reasoning processes (God-given common sense). This is best illustrated by the following anecdote.

A married couple were at home one evening when the telephone rang. The husband answered the call and was heard by his wife to say; "Mister, you have the wrong number; how in the world should I know anything about that—why don't you call the Coast Guard to find out?" After this short reply the husband hung up the phone, and was asked by his wife, "Who was that, dear?" The husband quickly replied, "Some jerk called here to ask if the coast was clear, and I told him to call the Coast Guard for that information."

From a completely objective point of view, absolutely nothing appeared improper to the husband, but the wife inductively knew differently. There was a hidden agenda and the husband could not perceive it. The truth was literally before his eyes and within his hearing if he had been at all suspicious of his wife and could correctly interpret the disquiet hint that was there.

For similar reasons, no one in the criminal justice system can avoid using inductive reasoning processes and lose these correlations, if the victims of criminal violence are to be adequately served.

7. This is an eye test that contains numerous, small colored circles, within which a large number or a letter is constructed. Only a colorblind person will not see the pattern.

8. If the victim is the only party injured at the scene of a crime and the perpetrator and victim have different blood types, whose body fluid can it be? Under the circumstances as the case is described, does anyone believe for one minute that it was the perpetrator who was dragged down that path, especially after the dead body of the babysitter was found downstream? At what confidence level can a crime laboratory report state the obvious? Any disassociation of this case from past experiences or future cases in crime scene examinations is thought (by the author) to be an unworthy activity by any prosecution expert.

9. The assailant was subsequently identified and arrested for this killing some weeks later while other police were investigating another, unrelated, distant crime. Good investigative methods and an alertness to other areas of need in the department brought otherwise "disassociated" circumstances together. Keeping only "to the rules" could never have accomplished this feat of induction; however, without "the rules," the induction would have been groundless and impossible.

See Chapter Seven and its footnote #4 (using deductive and inductive reasoning).

Chapter 10

THE EUREKA DISCOVERY

Ones' conviction that evidence is of real objective brand is only one more subjective opinion added to the lot.

—William James

The most formidable weapon against error of every kind is reason.

—Thomas Paine

A call was received by the police headquarters radio dispatcher that assistance was required at a two-story, single family residence regarding an accident that had occurred to one of the occupants in the home. In police parlance, this type of call is termed "an aided case" meaning that some type assistance is needed by the public and that no arrest is anticipated. All too often such cases can quickly turn out to be otherwise due to unexpected circumstances. This one was to follow that pattern also.

The radio dispatcher alerted the nearest radio motor patrol (RMP) car to respond to the address given to the police by the male voice seconds before with the added information that an ambulance from the nearest hospital was also being dispatched. Upon arrival, the two uniformed officers were greeted by a confused, grief-stricken male about thirty-five years of age. He quickly stated that his mother had been busy performing her normal household chores, specifically putting the freshly ironed family clothes away on the second floor, when the accident happened. As the three men entered the neat, one-family home, the

150

son stated that he had been seated in the family living room reading the sports page on this Tuesday morning, when suddenly there was a brief, sharp cry from above and the sound of his mother falling down the flight of stairs that led from the bedroom area on the second floor. He immediately went to her aid and found her crumpled at the foot of the stairs, a few feet from where he had been reading his newspaper. She was motionless when he found her and he immediately called the police for help from the kitchen phone.

"I knew she was dead immediately upon seeing her there on the floor," he blurted out to an unasked question. "My father and I warned her not to have throw rugs at the top of the stairs but she insisted that the beautiful wood floors in the house not be covered over with rugs."

As he was talking, one officer was sympathizing with appropriate head motions and questions while the second officer was quickly taking notes to the conversation, the son's story, and his replies to the questions, in short phrases which would be the text of their official report of the incident. These notes would be referred to many times in the future as the details of this "accident" become more formalized, eventually to take the form of a signed statement that the son would sign after noting any needed corrections. By the time the officers had heard the initial details, between gasps and tears, the ambulance, previously dispatched by the police operator, had arrived and the responding medical intern pronounced the middle-aged woman DOA. This was a sad, regrettable family tragedy—one of the many these officers had seen over their years of service and a scene that would be duplicated many times again in their careers. Since there was nothing of an emergency nature that the intern could do to aid the victim, this incident now became an "Investigation—DOA," which required the hospital personnel to leave the human remains at the scene for further police investigation.

Normal police procedures under these circumstances required that specific notifications be made to other units of the police department depending on what the officers developed from their skeptical inquiries and their observations of the total scene. There being no evidence of foul play, notifications that were sent out were limited to a confirmation to the local detective unit of an accidental death which in turn required that the detective "catching" during these last four hours of the tour respond to the scene of this investigation. Within the hour a detective from the same precinct as the responding officers arrived. Notification to other units such as homicide, crime laboratory, prosecutor's, and medical examiner's offices, and the need for additional assistance in manpower or other special needs were put off until this detective viewed what these officers believed to be true accidental death.

"No use to notify headquarters on this one," the junior officer said as the detective arrived, took off his raincoat, and opened his jacket. "It will save you an unusual." (A written report alerting senior police management of an unusual death or other serious circumstance. The report is to be sent to police headquarters as soon as possible, when required.)

It was now this detective's responsibility to view the scene and determine if it warranted further police investigation or for him to give society's final avowal and mark the police case closed. If the deceased had died from other than natural causes a routine autopsy would be performed at the medical examiner's office and the medical examiner would then sign the death certificate instead of the family doctor. The detective knew that any real need for the medical examiner should be picked up at this scene, if at all possible, and that was his job—to evaluate these needs and push or not push more buttons. It was this detective's job to look for a hidden agenda in this case, if there was one to be found. In order to do so, he must not allow himself to be stampeded into accepting situations that might be obvious to others. This officer is most often more experienced than those of the uniformed force who initially responded to the call for assistance and who had been only safeguarding the body pending his arrival and determination. The detective remembered all too well his tours "in the bag," the cold, the hot, the lonely tours of duty in uniform. "That was a while back and a lot of experience has been gained since then," he recalled as he mentally left the presence of the three other men in the room and started his survey of the scene, while continuing into a deeper concentration and self-interrogation.

He orientated himself to this scene by "walking through" the rooms looking at nothing in particular, but everything in general. He was simply being comprehensively curious of his surroundings. He became engrossed with the scene as he thought to himself, *Was there something here that should not be here or was there something missing from the scene that should be there?* He was well aware that anything that could arouse his suspicions could give the investigation a totally different direction. As his feet were doing the work of mechanically moving his large frame around the areas of the home, his mind continued to survey the area in order to try to understand the situation.

"In many ways it was certainly easier being a detective and, 'out of the bag' until you received a call like this," he mentally murmured to himself. He knew all too well that at times like this a negative report was always easier to write up than a positive one and that it certainly was tempting to do so now; *how many times had he heard that one,* he thought. There was a sort of personal pride that denied him this option as he reasoned, "After all, these victims had feelings, hopes, and desires, as I do, not too many hours ago—and now look at this poor woman," he reflected as he bent over to look for the source of the blood coming from the head of the deceased.

"Have you notified the house for a policewoman?" he inquired of one of the officers who was smoking nearby. Receiving the expected affirmative answer, he realized that his question had been asked only to fill the void of silence that hung in the room. He was supposed to be the leader now and ask intelligent questions, as if he really knew what he was doing and looking for.

He realized that he missed the mark on that one—these officers were experienced and, like himself, knew the proper sequences that needed to be followed even to the extent that one uniformed officer was still talking in a low murmur to the son of the deceased in a distant corner of the room; *Right on,* the detective thought. The deliberate distraction allowed the detective to view the scene undisturbed by questions or the physical presence of a concerned relative. He needed to view the entire scene so he could be completely familiar with it prior to formulating any additional questioning of the sole witness. He let his thoughts swarm and his impressions flit about without method or guide as he tried to determine the essential reality of the situation. As he did so, he reflected that the problem with police work was that every crime is different; names, places, faces, circumstances, motives, weather, and type of crime. These thoughts were flowing through his mind, soon to be crowded out by more troublesome thoughts. *If you only had more time—but no amount of time would really be enough,* he speculated as he surveyed the scene with the probing mind and, of course, the stairs—from the top to the bottom and up again. A throw rug, all crumpled up, was on the third step from the top of the stairwell; waxed floors and steps glistened up at him as he viewed them, noticing red, blood-like stains on several of the steps where she had hit her head on her way down; it sure was a long drop!

He was now in deep thought. *What makes these investigations hard is that the important turning points in any case are never obvious at first glance—no matter how hard you tried. Then, the standard "quick and dirty way" was the way to do it; look for the means, motive, and opportunity for it to be otherwise before you close a case out.* As he continued to view the scene he mentally laughed to himself—"Don't confuse me with facts" was the tired expression.

This could be an easy one—no one will check beyond my efforts because once I mark it closed, it stays closed and this scene just disappears like a fog at sunrise. If I do otherwise I had better be right—real right because it will cause a lot of people some trouble if I start to push those buttons unnecessarily, he mused as he moved about the house in wide-ranging circles. He was trying to picture in his mind (visualization) how it all happened or really could have happened. That was the secret to a good investigator—accept and deal with the challenge while keeping himself in an expectant mode. This professional could not be appeased with instant gratification so available to him nor could he be a robot. His mental chatter persisted. Everybody had a story to tell—you had to take it because they said it, and it was the only story immediately available. It was at least a place to start. You had to take it—but you don't have to believe it, at least not all of it right away.

I want to feel as if I accomplished something meaningful—I want to be more than just a pimple on the road to progress—there is a job to be done here and I'm now the one selected to make those decisions, he said to himself. *I can't let anyone put me in a convenient box and not allow me to use my experience and common sense to anticipate the possibilities that might coexist with the known facts, especially since there are no cookbook decisions to be made in any of these cases.*

He realized he was responding to a challenge when there might not be a challenge at all. *I cannot be value neutral* he thought, *if it should be otherwise. I have to look for the hidden potential using healthy skepticism.*

He continued to mentally argue with himself as he paused in his investigation, stepped outside the house unnoticed, and took a smoke on the rear steps that overlooked a neat, well-tended, fenced yard that in turn touched other fences as far as the eye could see. He began the painful thinking process of the investigation as he mixed up the events of the last hour in his mind. He mentally reflected that there was only one witness to this accident, and either the son was truthful or he was not. If he was telling the truth accurately there should be nothing at this scene that is out of the ordinary. If anything unsettling is found then the laws of substraction[1] would apply to the son since he was the sole witness to the accident. *How did it go? Potential is the justified expectations in the evidence, that is short of objective reality with no other reasonable alternatives.* The words were almost audible in his mind as he blew smoke and it was caught by the light breeze in the afternoon air. As he turned, he knew the story; now, being something of a realist who brings his conscience to work with him, he mentally posed the question, *If it did, how could it have happened otherwise? What might be here that was askew?* With a flick of his finger the cigarette flew into the garden and he turned and reentered the house and started down the rear basement steps, adjacent to the kitchen, only because it was the only portion of the house he had not yet seen. He was not being nosy, but wanted to be open to the possibilities of gaining new evidence, insights from any unobtrusive observations. He had to view the entire scene as the devil's advocate, questioning everything he was told or saw. There was always that need to question— that is why he was being paid the higher salary he eagerly accepted, constantly testing the known facts. Without that ability to think aggressively, to be a potent intermediary for society, he would be as useless as any jury that is supposed to function but without being given all the facts to consider.

The trial jury was there to second-guess him if he wasn't satisfied with the information he received. They were the final judges if things didn't fit the story given him. *I do the interpreting and unravel the mystery,* he thought. *They consider the facts and do the deciding if I find something wrong. An attorney can slash through any irrelevance to seize the main issue in a case but a good investigator can never have that luxury—it is all too easy to drift in the direction of least resistance and accept any plausible story.* He continued thinking. *A good investigator has to anticipate and not be too mechanical or preprogrammed—be more con-*

cerned with patterns than with minute details and just care a little. Very few cases are solved by the numbers because the numbers don't fit neatly and exactly all the time; these scenes are as untidy places as they are logical and bewildering. There are no high-tech solutions to this work, just common sense and a willingness to risk, if need be. The internal debate continued as he viewed the basement from the bottom step of the stairs leading down from the kitchen. Every investigation is like a horse race—everything is known at the beginning until just one new thing changes the odds and then you have a new horse race. He was looking for that one new thing and if he didn't find it the first time through the scene, he would start all over again until he satisfied himself that there was nothing more to be found!

In the basement all was normal and in place as far as he could see—a basement being a basement. He moved about in the well-lighted area thinking, *If only the basement or a small part of it were newly repaired in some corner or a new wall put in place, freshly painted—but it wasn't.* The scattered work tools on the work bench against the far wall were briefly examined for any red stains, but all looked normal and well used. The only item he couldn't inspect was the water drain, off-centered and towards one corner, in the concrete floor. *I wonder,* he mused as a flash of insight overcame him as he viewed what could be a discontinuity with the norm, the buried reality he was looking for. He went for a telephone in the first floor kitchen and called the police dispatcher telling him to get the laboratory over there—top priority. Before too many minutes had gone by other wheels in a distant part of the city started responding to this request for technical assistance.

The mobile crime laboratory team responded to the call and prepared to start processing the scene on the first and second floors before they or the detective, being in the basement, knew the other was there. Upon hearing voices and footfalls above him, the detective let out a yell that directed the lab technicians to the basement. Explaining his need to examine the contents of the drain to baffled faces, technical procedures were begun. Long glass pipettes were inserted through the drain metal cover, but these long glass tubes only sucked up air because they were too short. They didn't hit the bottom of the drain. The cover in the concrete surface was removed and the pipette was again inserted and lowered deeper into the cavity, then the glass tube filled with a cloudy, light tinted water. Of course there might not have been any water in there—but there was. It gave a positive reaction to the benzidine reagent—a quick, deep blue color. The detective was immediately cautioned by the laboratory technicians "that this was only a preliminary test for human blood;" the positive response seen could be in reaction to any kind of oxygen carrying substance—from any animal, dog, cat, chicken, or from the juices of some vegetables, but it could be—"And that, my friend," he said as he interrupted these experts in midsentence and reached his crest of resolution, "is the 'but' I have been looking for! I do not have to agonize over decisions like that."

For this officer, finding a positive reaction in the water where none should have been was identical to Locard's advice and was similar to Fleming's finding so many years ago. The total inconsistency of finding this reaction, under these conditions, could not be ignored. His response to this petty circumstance was not cold, impersonal, or inappropriate to the situation he had developed by being insightful and alert to the abnormal; he possessed an innate sense of the fitness of things and the water reaction didn't agree with that estimate, there was an intangible idea of genuine necessity, the recognition of latent, interlocking mechanisms that flowed from this discovery that felt true. It was critical thinking—a concerned act of interpolation and correlation of the incomplete evidence in the factual situation with a new reality, once some anomaly was noticed and a confident projection made. Under any other circumstances it would have been little more than an intuitive stumble. However, in these instances the effective significance was comprehended by an alert mind that reflected skill, trust, and courage in solving the problem. He had recognized what would otherwise have been the wasted potential in the evidence. This investigator had found and recognized the hidden agenda that was to have been kept from him.

Hours later, after the case had passed from the initial investigative stage to the accusatory stage due to this finding and when further, more directed questioning had been done, the aura of innocence surrounding the distraught witness was shattered when a confession to the killing was obtained from the son of the deceased. A new story unfolded that filled in the voids that had arisen in the mind of the investigating detective hours before. The mother and son had had bad feelings about his not getting a job after being laid off several months ago and for the late hours he was starting to keep. In recent weeks and with increased frequency, voices and tempers escalated as each tried to justify their opinions to each other. The argument resurfaced again this particular day as soon as the son appeared for another late breakfast. To avoid another heated discussion on the same old subject, the son had retreated to the basement to avoid this further bantering only to have his mother follow him in her continual nagging. In a rage of blind anguish, almost in an orgasm of hate that was comprehensively human, he quickly grabbed the first heavy object nearby and hit her, once over the head, with a metal carpenter's level. Death immediately followed as the mother's body slumped to the floor. A story was quickly put together by the son that would explain this accidental death to the authorities and, who was to say otherwise since there were no other witnesses? The body was taken to the second floor of the home and allowed to free fall down the wooden steps. This clever deception would add bruises to the body and give credibility to the fatal injuries. The basement was cleared of all signs of any struggle and the bloodstains on the floor from the attack were washed down the sewer drain.

Many things could have allowed this case to remain an "aided case" such as if the investigator had not been conscientious; if the drain had been a dry well, or a drain without any water in it, if the reagent used was not as sensitive as it is; if the detective had used only deductive reasoning, accepted only the obvious and gone no further, accepting the first story given to him by the grieving, loving son; if the detective had failed to accept his serious responsibilities especially when there was no one else to know otherwise; if he had been like so many others that believed themselves fated to lose and therefore (subjectively) incapable of making the struggle; if the detective had less compassion for the victims of a violent crime; if the investigator had not used relevant imagery to unearth the hidden agenda; if the examiner, using shrewd judgment, had not tried to make a legitimate leap in logic and ignored the incomplete evidence *that was there*, as is done in so many other cases.

What seems to be needed in so many of these cases is to have sympathetic thinking that leaps over a logical gap, that postulates and backfills the empty spaces (a gestalt closure) using a sense perception of sure confidence in these and in past experiences of value, the logical, reasonable implications in the necessary connections presupposed to be present. A rational option to explain the circumstances which demand that the specific disquiet reality be called forth. The greatest failure is the ignorance that when these natural voids or interruptions do occur that there is an inherent integrity, a continuity in them, that they are not irrelevant complications or arbitrary exceptions, just scattered about.

There seems to be a severe inability to fully value and comprehend the situation and the attached serendipitous, collateral, latent, incomplete evidence waiting to be found. We must not dodge our chosen responsibilities by failing to give voice to these reasonable expectations, the meaningful realisms that refuse to be pushed aside, the truth, when we know we know it. We must have complete confidence in the principles taught to us by Locard and Fleming and so many others and believe in them and cease to remain technical porcupines using only fixed, safe, reflex technology. In all aspects of life it is always a difficult task to deal with that which is less than certain but for an authentic criminalist it is an issue he cannot avoid because the search for truth forces him to be inductive in every criminal case. He must constantly solve this problem or be professionally devoured by it. It then follows automatically, in all cases and circumstances, that to support any cause is to expose its ends—and that to believe in it—is to care and then to care is to do.

MEANINGFUL DISCLOSURES

1. All things being equal, if all but one witness can be eliminated from immediate serious concern, a logical and reasonable consequence then follows that the remaining person's activities need additional close in-depth scrutiny. This might reveal circumstances thought to be worthy of prosecutor, grand jury, or trial jury considerations. This method of problem solving will only be worthwhile if inductive reasoning methods, argument by reflection, are understood and acted upon.

Chapter 11

HEROES FOR THE PROSECUTION

*Our system faces no theoretical dilemma but a single continous problem;
how to apply the ever changing conditions to the never changing principles of
freedom*

—Chief Justice Earl Warren
U.S. Supreme Court

*Reconciliation of the irreconcilable, merger of antitheses, the synthesis of
opposites, these are the great problems of the law. These are the great problems
of any scientific discipline*

—Associate Justice Benjamin Cardoza
U.S. Supreme Court

At about the time that the W.S.P. hit-and-run vehicle homicide
case was winding down, another homicide trial was being concluded some twenty-five hundred miles away that demonstrated
more clearly what can be done with circumstantial evidence. To
properly do so requires competency, compassion and a willingness
"to stand up and be counted" when such information is found.

The tragic circumstances had started five years before with
the deaths of the three members of U.S. Army Captain Jeffrey
MacDonald's family, namely his wife and two daughters, in the
morning hours of February 17, 1970. It was to take almost five
years of extended effort to bring the case to trial. This long delay
was due to a combination of factors but principally due to the
poor performance of evidence-handling procedures by units of
the U.S. Army prior to the initial inquiry hearings in 1970. Evi-

dence had been mishandled, lost, and the crime scene poorly searched and safeguarded, and the evidence that was there was not assimilated. As happens all too often a diffusion of responsibility occurs when there is not a close working relationship among the investigators, crime scene search teams, and the crime laboratory servicing the area.

The crime scene was a small one-family house on the open military post of Fort Bragg, North Carolina. The small abode had been a classic crime scene, countless items of circumstantial evidence waiting to be found if viewed in a concerned manner. If this is not done, only chaos results and the victims are left unserved. It was not done in this case and the initial charges against the accused were dismissed due to insufficient evidence. Since the crimes had been committed within a military jurisdiction all the evidence was processed by military personnel and it was to take almost five years before a civilian court was to take notice of the injustice. In 1975, a grand jury was to indict and a trial jury convict Dr. MacDonald of these three deaths. To a large extent the circumstantial evidence at the scene was only uncovered after the FBI was given jurisdiction months later, and much too late for the initial proceedings in 1970.

The serendipitous, happy event was the eventual recognition that all four of the main participants, Dr. MacDonald, his wife Colette, and two children all had different blood types (four out of four), which is most unusual, especially for a family of that size. The activities of each member could be traced, "seen" by any interested party who took the time and cared to look. The army CID investigators realized that the minor wounds to Dr. MacDonald and his activities at the crime scene were seriously questionable, but their suspicions were unsupported by the lack of circumstantial evidence until the FBI became involved. The injuries suffered by the female members of the family were extensive and totally out of proportion to those suffered by the strongest, most prominent, most potentially dangerous, the single male member of the family, Captain MacDonald. The physical damages

163

to the living room area where four assailants assaulted Captain MacDonald was minimum and none of his blood was found in the premises. The most important circumstantial piece of evidence (there were others) was a black pajama top worn by Dr. Mac-Donald and supposedly used by him as a shield to fend off repeated stab attacks from his assailants. The same pajama top was eventually found to be on the body of Mrs. MacDonald in their master bedroom. Mrs. MacDonald, in addition to many other wounds and broken bones, had been stabbed twenty-one times with an ice pick. The forty-eight holes in the black pajama top matched the wounds in Mrs. Colette MacDonald's body (and her pink pajama top) indicating that the black pajama was actually covering her, in an unsupported fashion, at the time she received the blows. Dr. MacDonald denied that the family kept an ice pick as a kitchen utensil only to be refuted by several witnesses who had previously visited the home as invited guests and actually used the pick in the home. There were other similar important inconsistencies that went unnoticed in the original crime scene search procedures.

The harmful evidence that was eventually brought to light in a courtroom had always been at the crime scene and only awaited the receptive mind and attention of a proactive professional to give it meaning. To surface and give opinion evidence and absorb the anticipated heat from the defense attorney took the painful thinking, courage and fortitude of an authentic criminalist. Without this willingness to be inductive and forthright, the victims and concerned relatives would not have been vindicated nor would justice have been served.

Another outstanding case demonstrating the turn of events in a criminal case, solely due to the professionalism of the expert, was the Cappalino homicide investigation. Without the use of inductive logic, and the externalizing of subjective professional obligations of the prosecution expert regardless of any personal discomfort, this case too would have been lost and no one would have known otherwise. This concerned the testimony of Dr. Milton Helpern, New York City Chief Medical Examiner. Once again a sham was prevented from happening because the disquiet reality, the evidence that revealed the deliberately concocted hidden agenda was not overlooked.

The case involved a New Jersey anesthesiologist, Dr. Carl Cappalino, who was accused of killing a New Jersey neighbor in September 1963, and his wife Carmello in Florida in August 1965. In both cases, it was suspected that death was brought on from massive injection of succinylcholine chloride, a drug essentially used in anesthesiology. When it is administered by injection during an operation it requires close medical supervision because the drug causes deliberate and immediate respiratory paralysis in the patient as medically required. This requires immediate auxiliary respiratory support on the part of attending medical personnel to artificially support the collapsed breathing mechanism of the patient. In the absence of this necessary assistance, immediate paralysis of the automatic nervous system occurs, quickly bringing on death. In Carmello Cappalino's case, a single hypodermic puncture wound was found at autopsy with no other signs of anatomical, fatal physical injuries, or contributing factors for her death. The normally administered drug succinylcholine chloride cannot be found in the human body at autopsy even in persons to whom it is known to have been given therapeutically during an operation. Normally such a medication would not be noticed, except in a directed autopsy and then only the "innocent" and innoxious separated chemical breakdown products of succinic acid and chlorine can be identified and these chemicals by themselves would not cause death. Only by inductively *reuniting* these breakdown products to the parent drug when found at autopsy in the absence of any other reason for death (law of substraction) in an otherwise healthy individual; only by being astutely aware of this medically known continuity and of his obligations to the victim, could Dr. Halpern have given his professional findings and damning interpretative expert testimony against the accused. He presented this sophisticated information to a criminal court jury for their consideration and judgment.[1]

Very few experts would have exposed themselves to that extent knowing full well the expected onslaught from the defense, but that is what such heroes are made of when, through their expertise, they are able to professionally overcome the technical imperfections in the evidence by explaining the mitigating circumstances to a jury. The victim's need and society's desire for justice and retribution in the presence of such evidence is recognized and this necessity to expose the truth is far superior to any personal discomfort on the part of such dedicated experts. However, such acts of initiative are few and far between, even unpalatable to most other professionals, and their cherished objectivity and detachment is allowed to hide and overcome the true reality so often present in many other criminal investigations.

A third case comes to mind that further documents the theme. In the northwestern sector of Washington State there is a very picturesque area known as the San Juan Islands. On one of these islands, Lopez Island, a startling criminal trial was beginning in the fall of 1985 that had few legal precedents in criminal law. The events that can only be described as dramatic surround the attempt by San Juan prosecutor's office to prosecute a person for the first-degree murder of a ship's captain. This unusual homicide trial was to consider the strange surroundings in the death of Capt. Rolf Neslund, although his body was never found.

Many people in the secluded town of Friday Harbor asked themselves, "How the hell can you prosecute somebody when you don't have any evidence?" The San Juan County prosecutor's office admitted that the case was not an easy one to prosecute since they had no body; "It's harder to prosecute, but it can be done" was one estimate given to the inquiring reporters who crowded into the small courthouse in this vacation paradise just north of the Emerald City of Seattle, Washington.

166

The defendant was an elderly woman who had recently suffered a stroke and was now legally blind. She and her husband owned and operated a bed and breakfast resort and she was being charged in his death. Capt. Rolf Neslund had been a ferry boat captain for many years and with his gracious wife, Ruth, retired to this laid back community by purchasing an old house on Lopez Island in 1976.

The legal process had begun years before the trial when Rolf was suspected to have been shot by his wife in an argument over money. The prosecution maintained that the body was dismembered and completely burned in a barrel and that no body parts were found. The prosecution had produced crime laboratory reports of human blood stains found at the scene but it was acknowledged that both husband and wife had the same blood type. The state's case depended upon the testimony of close relatives of Ruth Neslund, who stated that at various times in conversations with Ruth, she described the gruesome circumstances.

The defense strongly maintained that the captain was not deceased, but had planned a trip to Norway and was never to return. His car was found at the local ferry dock giving the impression that a trip had taken place.

The prosecution was keenly aware that "there weren't many cases nationwide where there had been a conviction with no body." The state's attorney, Greg Conova, assisted by Charles Silverman, also realized that it was a jury decision and the jury did "an incredibly thorough, conscientious job and did what the evidence indicated they should have done." Mrs. Ruth Neslund was found guilty as charged.

When the jury was asked after the trial as to how they reached their unanimous verdict, one juror replied, "It was not the decision we would like to have reached but the evidence was too much."

Another said, "It was one thing on top of another on top of another."

And still another said, "No one element of the evidence was the key to the conviction. Each one of us had different things that weighed on it—it was everything. We went through everything."

The jury simply believed the prosecution and not the defense. The prosecution developed a more persuasive approach in the use of circumstantial evidence and presented the information to the jury. The conviction in the first degree meant that the jury believed the prosecution's contention that the murder occurred and was premeditated. They are the ultimate decision makers of facts, the community's conscience.

In the very brief review of three homicide cases, each separated by time, circumstances, and distance, we have observed a criminalist, a pathologist, and a prosecutor perform the difficult tasks that society had delegated to them to solve. Each in their own area of specialization had accepted the challenge that circumstances beyond their control had selected them to consider, each in their official capacities, to render technical opinions with at least reasonable probability (or higher) of being right. Such "experts" must first notice the possibilities (the possible existence of a hidden agenda) and then comprehend the high correlations, the unlocking realizations, the significant potentials that deal with cause and effect, the integrated truth that is rationally and logically predictable as grim realism when initiated by them, if they will but try, if they will but use a different game plan. Through their efforts, created tensions were developed in the evidence; an urgency, an idea of genuine necessity that only they could have developed and only a jury decide. To dare to do so, these experts had to overcome their initial fears, act responsibly and not remain elegantly detached from the situation.[2] Compassion for the victims brings to a conclusion the endless clash of theories and forces the true professional to become involved and not remain aloof from the calculated, technically dirty conclusions[3] demanded in order to express the inferred truth from the incomplete evidence.

Had Paul Stombaugh, Dr. Halpern, or Greg Canova not seen the internal couplings, the mitigating circumstances—had they not had the professional courage, the moral stamina to speak out, had they not become the critical catalysts that the victims and juries needed—these homicides would never have been solved. Without using inventive synthesis as the absolute fulcrum in these cases, these cases would never have been subject to judicial review. The latent evidence, the disquiet realities, were gentle but insistent and the victims would have remained voiceless and powerless[4] if a compassionate concern for them had not been expressed in a court of law by these heroes for the prosecution.

The critical information for jury impact (the nail for the horse's shoe) will be lost and remain unconnected if the expert does not recognize the natural, impersonal, synergistic consequences at points of accidental interruptions as seen in so many criminal cases.[5] The solutions reach out beyond the hollow ring of statistics and permit the jury to shape a civilized solution because the authentic experts did not ignore the implications perceptible in the evidence. Without such stimulation from the prosecution experts, many injustices will go unnoticed. The experts in these three cases had to use inductive observations and respond in the absence of eyewitnesses, firm or risk free objective facts or concerns to prove the cases beyond a scientific doubt. They responded to the integrity of the disquiet order that did exist in the evidence and made use of the unexpected event by using insight and comprehensive integration of the imperfect evidence (sound perception), and gave a voice to the otherwise invisible collateral components most often avoided by persons of less character and personal involvement. These experts exposed "the naked truth" for jury consideration by making available what appeared to the layman to be unassimilable facts into astute declarations, given as intellectually honest evaluations of the reality, the crude truth in the criminal cases under study. These experts live at the edge of their accomplishments and acknowledge the ethical imperatives and linkages seen so often in the imperfect evidence. These individuals did not have judicial pessimism, clouded vision, anemic will, or failure of nerve. These individuals exercised their incumbent professional options to make a legitimate leap in logic for the benefit of the crime victims. Such individuals are today almost an extinct species much to society's detriment due to poor present day crime laboratory management policies.[6]

In all similar instances, we must live with the constant expectations of our observations, that the natural order is functioning (voids included); for to do otherwise, we would have to retract and deny as unbelievable all the historical scientific circumstances and the order we have come to know in so many other instances and this we must not, cannot do. A gross miscarriage of justice follows whenever any investigator ignores these factors. If we do deny this supreme order, our only alternative is to stop in our tracks, deny inductive reasoning in the biased evidence and our personal experiences. The victims pay the extreme price for our passive approach to the solutions needed. This is exactly what is being fallaciously done to so many thousands of cases.

The law itself and the police powers of the state are being perverted in many of these criminal cases. The law is being turned from its proper purpose and made, by the default of its own experts, to follow an entirely contrary purpose because "we the people" have lost our capacity for indignation. We in reality are now doing little more than rearranging the chairs on the *Titanic* and allowing these released culprits to strike again and again. The all too few experts that do use inductive reasoning are well aware that each new case is not a totally unique phenomenon. All previous criminal cases are like history—a lived reality—from which they did learn something from each case and from this reservoir of developed knowledge, justified influences and critical connections can be expected! A sense of proportion between the voids and the many facts (in the vast majority of criminal investigations) can be established if the concerned experts will internalize their experiences and not be polarized into fixed positions. The experts in these three homicide investigations are as totally involved in their professions as any of the elitists who are censured in these pages. The difference is that, to their lasting credit, these three exerted themselves and dealt with reality by interpreting the theoretical constructs of their chosen professions and brought that information down to the space "where the tire meets the roadway" in these cases. Each fully realized that almost any set of circumstances was possible but that it was highly improbable, virtually impossible that an accidental coincidence could have occurred in these situations; that their information and observations were trustworthy. They understood that a *cause and effect relationship* did exist and that they were conscience bound to express these concerns to the triers of fact, to fulfill the juries' truth finding obligations. They were mission effective. It is the rare exception when this is attempted or allowed elsewhere in modern day criminalistics although, as we have seen, it can be done and is absolutely essential to do so.

MEANINGFUL DISCLOSURES

1. The entire episode concerning this case must be considered in at least two complicated parts in which, to his undying credit, Dr. Halpern, acting in his professional capacity, actively took part in both events.

The first phase concerned the death investigation in New Jersey thought to have been committed by the administration of some drug. Due to the efforts of an aggressive defense attorney (who was doing his job as such), the defendant was judged by a trial jury to be "not guilty" due to mitigating factors that helped "cloud the real issues" in the case. Undaunted by this "initial failure," Dr. Halpern testified against the same defendant in the second part of this episode in Florida. With complete knowledge that he would again face the same aggressive defense attorney (who was forewarned since he had possession of all the technical information of the first trial) considering the same type of evidence, Dr. Halpern "stuck to his guns" on the exact same theory as in the first case in New Jersey, minus the mitigating circumstances of the first case and a conviction was obtained. Unlike Mark Twain's cat, Dr. Halpern was not hesistant to again place his head "above the parapets" for the sake of a second victim and this time sit on a cold stove. This could only have been done by a person who is the epitome of a forensic expert and one who was given the administrative support needed when he was (figuratively) bloodied at the first trial!

It is absolutely impossible to perform society's assigned task of being a proactive prosecution expert without both ingredients being present.

Dr. Halpern did not turn away from his duty (as did the off-duty police officer in Chapter 7 and Kitty Genovese's neighbor in Chapter 9) or from what he had to view as at least an expected, unpleasant experience in his Florida appearance. He could have "lost" again in court; he could have easily avoided any of these confrontations for his entire career by not preparing himself to see the hidden agendas as so many of us have done, and no one would have known otherwise. This was the positive side of the "toy gun syndrome"! This is the only acceptable performance by men of conscience reflecting the principles of Christian humanism. See Chapter Thirteen and its footnote #5.

2. Every expert has fears of possibly being wrong but we cannot be paralyzed by this fear or by an equally human concern—that of being ridiculed and "raked over the coals" by any defense attorney when he does his job of defending the accused in a court of law.

3. These are individuals who are not dealing with intellectual abstractions but with (moral & ethical) irritations of conscience

in real situations. Those are decisions demanded by conscience that require a reasonable, coherent leap in logic—an "unprofessional leap" that most others will refuse to even acknowledge exists, or worse, deride those who will. In not making these decisions, the courts remain blind to the hidden agendas that are deliberately constructed to hide the truth in so many criminal situations.

4. Like a five-year-old child whose parents are in the final processes of divorce, the child is torn with anxiety, totally involved but not at all in control of events; totally left out, with no voice concerning the outcome that intimately affects him the most.

The victims of violent crimes are in an identical position as the child when they appeal to the criminal justice system to unravel their situations. If the system is a monopoly with no appeal processes for the victims and if the system does not respond to the victims' needs in a meaningful fashion, the victim is likewise totally helpless within the very system he depends on for support. The accused is assured a fair trial and an appeal process from any guilty verdict to assure that he has received due process under the law. The victim has no such appeal procedures if his case is pushed aside or ignored by those in the system and few seem to care for it to be otherwise.

5. The principles espoused by Locard and Fleming, et al. (that the needed solutions can be well within the locus of our control), are as true today as they were when first verbalized, and they continue to be so.

6. Since the pressure to perform always runs downhill, the direct consequence of "zero error" and to prove a technical criminal case "beyond a scientific doubt" is to managerially suffocate any desire on the part of the analyst to risk anything, under any circumstances, and it encourages redundancy in test procedures to assure that level of performance. This is nothing less than unconstrained pedantic protocol (cookbook chemistry) to the det-

riment of all concerned. For the subordinate, when such a belief system is enforced (as in Arizona), the analyst must take a defensive position since they will not obtain administrative support if they make any mistakes. These analysts have become individuals who can "look at a beautiful bank of trees and see only lumber or read a page of profound poetry and see only the words"; the timber in the forest is seen and the words on the page read without insight, without weight, without profit and without any attempt at understanding; there will be no attempt to develop any proficiency in structural visualization and creative thinking techniques that would have been so helpful in the many types of criminal cases depicted in these pages; these passive workers have their eyes shut tight against even a glimpse of any new possibilities and the concomitant responsibilities to the innocent victims!

Chapter 12

SEEKING A SOLUTION

How can we insist on certainty when all we have in every day life are probabilities?
—Chief Justice Learned Hand
U.S. Court of Appeals

In this world nothing is said to be certain except death and taxes.
—Benjamin Franklin

As we live our lives we all find ourselves faced with the responsibilities of life as it has developed around us. Each of us is called to respond to these responsibilities and at times, because we are human, we hesitate because there are no guarantees that "the waters" will not be too deep or that we will avoid disaster or disappointment. We know that it is safer not to risk, to remain with the known and the familiar. We will usually not venture or extend ourselves from that which is safe, familiar, and stable unless we know it is a sure thing. To do the minimum is safest. We are the only creatures on this earth allowed to make these choices because nature forces compliance and completion on all other creatures and systems. Being the unique creatures we are in this universe, we have been given responsibilities that must be met if we are to be at peace with our surroundings. Only with the serious acceptance of our unique responsibilities comes the strength and the compassion that permits us to accept risk. Only when we are willing to risk, will we by comparison see that we have most often been dealing only with the inconsequentials in our lives and are now ready to sail into the deep and fulfilling waters of accomplishment. We are then no longer just timid dabblers or guilty bystanders.

In working out these internal demands we cannot be like a linguist caught up in the fascination of analyzing speech patterns without ever understanding that the text could be communicating an urgent message. Nor can we be like Mark Twain's cat, who having suffered and then learned not to sit on a hot stove, refuses thereafter to ever again sit on any other stove—hot or cold. Therefore we need to be alert and at least be open to the risks in our lives and not avoid these opportunities because we might, as humans, make mistakes. The acceptance of these individual responsibilities is especially acute when we realize that it is we who, as individuals, are called and that there really is no one else to respond and do what needs to be done! As we live out our destinies, we must internalize, accept, and convert these facts of life to our individual surroundings. It is then, as criminalists, that we will realize that it is we who, in pursuing our careers, often have the needed information in criminal cases and we cannot escape our concomitant responsibilities to meaningfully communicate justifiable solutions to these problems to be the criminal courts whenever possible. That is the essence of the profession.

It is obvious that to be totally objective in our decisions is safest but it is also cold and uncaring, lifeless, joyless, unethical, and we can lose the opportunity to serve and the fulfillment that can come from the larger subjective use of our talents. The implications oozing out of the evidence can be lost if we reject these instances to perform. In processing the many types of criminal activities, there are times when this objectivity is not enough to fill the voids that become so apparent to us, and we need to prudently risk in order to meet our professional responsibilities. In our willingness to exhibit compassion and to deal with this reality at our risk, we will find the nettle or nugget that is there and realize that it must be seized if we, as experts for the prosecution, are to have a meaningful, personal existence. In doing so we must use caution, restraint, and good judgment. In these situations, it is we who must do it; we must seize it, move into it, and live with it. Criminalists must be, after all, activists and not spectators if the criminal justice system is to succeed in its purposes.

In order to verbalize our attitudes and maximize our capabilities we must develop a flexible decision matrix that expresses our desires and alternatives similar to any paint density gradient or wide-range prism, from the least to the most likely. The expressed probabilities are words used to describe inescapable latent implications and relationships that aid us and others to understand the essential nature of the present reality as we experienced it and its impact on the scene we are investigating; such inductive probability is a mediating link between the incomplete evidence (as usually found at a crime scene/case) and ethical reality since such an outward expression is a sign of an inward accord that would go unnoticed by the general public. We must have trust in the process and to the sensitivity that arises within us as a compelling logic, an inner reality that we have already experienced, similar to the other intangibles in life—love, conviction, and justice. We cannot be more concerned with rituals, authority, and structures than we are for mission, reality, and duty. We must do much more than just subject ourselves to those objective truths that our consciences may comfortably assimilate. Easy abdication of our responsibilities cannot be a road for us. The remedy is to insist on the consideration and inclusion of the obviously incomplete evidence and any hesitation or distaste to do so is but a traditional survival mechanism not appropriate for the prosecutor's expert.

In order to properly assimilate the truth there must be developed a workable strategy for constructive engagement with this reality, which will prevent a paralysis of our legal system.

Whatever system is developed to deal with the incomplete evidence as it exists in so many criminal cases, it must acknowledge and deal with the fact that that which is necessary must prevail over that which is excellent in any hierarchy of values and that there will be an element of risk that we must deal with and make known to the triers of fact. The motivating factor behind such activity is the total realization that the authentic criminalist has responsibilities to the victims of criminal violence and to the courts that are not intangible, that it is sheer arrogance (except in Arizona) to ever indicate that mistakes are never made and it is imperative that the laboratory reports exhibit common sense and uncommon courage. Whatever risks do exist are minimized due to the fact that in the biased evidence found at any scene there is no perversity, no haphazard collection of possibilities, no random data, nor any subterfuge. The biased evidence found does not lose its integrity because it is incomplete or indirect and such imperfect evidence need not be kept in isolation unnoticed, unattended, unused and untouchable. These efforts assisting law enforcement to become more effective are more than a contribution; it is a commitment, that only terminates at trial.

The trial process is a means by which we resolve our disputes. At the heart of the process is "the search for truth"! If this search, however, is not realized to the greatest extent possible, the jury, as agents of the general will, cannot perform its duties as triers of the facts and the victims are left wanting. The suggested use of subjective probability is the acknowledgment by the expert of a personal illumination, an inner responsibility, a deeply felt demand; it allows the expert to respond to a coherent reality, to harmonize with this reality; to reflect on it and to value it. The stated subjective probability is the expert's satisfaction of his subjective decision and is a weight indicating the sum total seen in the muted but cogent evidence in a sincere effort to make the truth more visible to a jury.

A conscientious criminalist, one with experience, integrity, conviction, and skill will use analytical probability to deal constructively with the disturbing truth and leverage his knowledge to the advantage of the victims, in their silent plea for assistance. This expression is more than sheer knowledge, it is the fulfillment of our obligation that is a justified, contributive expression of the expectation in the disquiet evidence, short of objective reality, with no reasonable alternative to do otherwise. Intuitive probability is no more than a codification of the realities confronting any investigator who dares to avoid willful ignorance and instead uses penetrating observations in his crime scene analyses. It is the expression of the logic of facts and events seen in the evidence. It is synonymous to the "Eureka" exclamation of Archimedes, but much heavier. At this stage we are above the "boiler plate" type of examinations and the subsequent written report must reflect the determination to reveal the latent truth so often left ignored. The pertinent conclusion is both the commonality usually expected and the variations that become noticeable when viewed by an inquiring, interactive mind. This is the paradox of the all too normal condition; each type of crime is at once the same and yet altogether different. The laws of nature, controlled roulette, guarantee distinctiveness from the moment the crime is committed. The case of inductive probability is the expression of the hidden potential, the unseen but necessary relationships, the unfinished unity, the unlocking realizations in the evidence. It is a survival, tactical choice interacting with the technical environment, however imperfectly programmed due to circumstances. The use of subjective probability is a metaphor for identification and interpretation, translating experiences and reasonable anticipations, expectations or educated projections into realdity-adjusted jargon. The use of subjective probability is both polemic and a practical guide, not a neurotic outcropping of our technical helplessness, but an integrating system that expresses our strong belief in orthodoxy and tradition, which in turn alows its mentors to extend themselves beyond the normal limits of the more timid practitioner.

This strong belief in a rational order allows us to extrapolate and triumph over naturally occurring voids. It is a new logic of power for the victims and once accepted, a lot of unfamiliar (not new) ideas follow. It is a social conscience expressing an ethical imperative reflecting a basic reality as it perceives the interconnectedness, the tight couplings in the viewed evidence, and is able to give reasonable value judgments to an empaneled jury. It is an external action that expresses an internal spirit, a disposition and conviction as integrated truth. Analytical probability contemplates the compelling predictability in the evidence and contemplates this tension between reality and the ideal. It is an effort to prevent the victims from being disenfranchised from the needed decisions they require only because the evidence itself is less than perfect. Without such a scheme to deal more effectively with this ever-present reality, it would be impossible to make an informed decision except under perfect circumstances and then we would remain pseudoparalyzed in our professional responses to this imperfect evidence and to these victim's needs. Our present mode of selective seeing is, in most cases, not due to any lack of evidence in the case. We fail to see out of fear of what we will be expected to do if we acknowledge this deeper awareness of the possibilities present in the incomplete evidence. The conceit for "zero error in all things" and that risk-free "certainty" that can be obtained prevents any case learning to occur or even a glimpse of the lesser possibilities in other cases, regardless of how close to the surface this truth reality might be. We alone have the power to make these technical decisions—if we, as processors of reality, really desire not to avoid our chosen responsibilities as experts for the criminal courts. Ultimate truth, which is the object of our search, can be supported using subjective probability as a means for the technical expert to extend his

180

intelligence and be open to the many subtle dimensions in the submitted but incomplete evidence. It permits us to introduce to trial juries, case clarifications, and describe instances of "the smoking gun syndrome" so often seen in the criminal evidence. These serendipitous situations are much more than mere credible coincidences and they will not cease occurring just because we do not understand or describe them; they will continue but go on unnoticed, uninterpreted, and continue to mock us with their silent laughter. If there is a willingness to tell the truth, the words of Andrew Hamilton during the Peter Zenger trial of 1735 might take on additional meaning, namely, "If it is not the law it is better than the law, it ought to be the law, and will always be the law wherever justice prevails."

INFORMATIVE REPORTING

When the expert uses inductive probability, such probability is insightful, interconnected persuasive information, forming a bridge of associations that reflect an inner significance of the events, with risk assessments concerning the dynamism that nature perpetuates with great integrity. This allows an endless stream of dilemmas to be faced and then resolved when presented to and considered by a trial jury. To do so we must have an irresistible compulsion to act effectively and consciously abandon inadequate customs and develop initiatives to do more with the less we are forced to work with and not be shunted into silence. We have as professional examiners a duty to participate that is an obligation of conscience.

As a member of a jury evaluating a criminal case, each juror has a personal threshold of believability that is a cumulative index and above this personal, imaginary line, he, as one individual, confidently believes that the state has proven the accused guilty beyond a reasonable doubt. It is an internal decision gradient not at all unlike a Richter Scale equivalent.[1] If this personal believability level is 85 percent (8.5 percentile) and the state's case exceeds that confidence level, the juror would vote for conviction of the accused based on this elevated measure of persuasion or on this more reasonable expectation of guilt. (It is an absolute in law that the state has the burden to prove the case beyond a reasonable doubt and such is accomplished if the individual jurors' threshold of believability is individually met.) When this is done, the defense automatically did not prove the accused not guilty in the eyes of this same juror more than 15 percent (1.5 percentile) of the time.

These values (85/15) do fluctuate independently and are mutually interdependent. Only one value need move (the prosecution) and, in so doing, automatically creates or eliminates the opposite value at least by default. (It is absolute in law that the accused does not even have to put up a defense but stand mute— but this does rebel against all common sense to do so and allows the state's aggregate case to build more quickly in the void. This is a valued defense option.)

The testimony of the prosecution expert is a juror-weighted ingot on their subjective and cumulative scales of justice. The prosecution's scale reading would be delinquently smaller if such prosecution testimony is in any manner diminished, not given, or is avoided for selfish reasons. Therefore, in order for the victims to be adequately represented, testimony must be given whenever possible and not limited to that which is obviously certain, conclusive, or to expert opinions that are too timid considering the evidence available. Such testimony in itself need not surpass the individual juror's threshold value (85 percent or 8.5), but be an important segment that cumulatively builds towards that critical flash point of believability (as in any decision gradient) above which the juror is persuaded beyond a reasonable doubt of the guilt of the accused. The expressed expert's analytical probability statement simply stresses whether, for him, the truth

182

is closer to one pole or another and to what degree. It is entirely up to each individual juror to decide if the totality of all the presented evidence is so clear and convincing that it has reached a point, for him as a prudent individual and juror, that is beyond a reasonable doubt. It is an act of judgment identical to the theme that exists when a person views the rising water level behind a reservoir after a bad storm (it having many contributories that add their ingredients to the rising level) or decides whether a glass of milk offered to him is a full glass. Only a glutton would insist that the glass (or the reservoir) must be "brim full" before he decides and acknowledges that he has received a full glass. Likewise, it is never necessary for the prosecution to convince any juror that the total aggregate of the evidence in any criminal case must reach what could be considered as an overwhelming level of belief before a guilty verdict can be reached.

An active defense of the accused needs to persuade this same juror to believe his client innocent only above the 15 percent (1.5 percentile), thereby automatically forcing the jurors' threshold of believability for conviction, to any point below the needed 85% (8.5 percentile) for that same juror. Such a reasonable doubt or low measure of persuasion must then be translated into a verdict of "not guilty" for that juror. The reservoir or the glass of milk is notably and unacceptably far less than full for this juror in this specific instance.[2]

To establish the validity of inductive logic and your own thresholds of believability, consider the following criminal case and how clear it is to subjectively determine a person's guilt, using our common sense, reasonableness and the "on board computer" we call conscience.

Memory recalls a case in which a horrified husband notified police that a night burglary of their home had resulted in the death of his wife as she broke free of her bonds and ran for help. "She had tried to flee to obtain help for me and the burglar shot her," he said in a tearful voice. There were no other witnesses for the police to question. Upon further examination police found the items listed as stolen from the home hidden in a U-Store-It facility over which the husband had sole custody. The rental contract, which was found in the home, had been signed by the husband the week before the "burglary."

Common sense and reflective intelligence (endogenous) show premeditation and guilt even though total deductive objectivity is missing since there was only one witness to the event. The subjective, inductive probability is very high that the accused killed his wife, sight unseen. There has to be an enormous contradiction, an immoral blindness, if the unambiguous and subliminal information contained in this and so many other similar cases, is rejected because the reasonableness that the necessary and sufficient elements are present is very strong. In using inductive logic and expressing these thoughts in a predictive probability matrix, we are acknowledging a behavioral interrelationship between action—reaction and a resultant (the elephant—the smoking gun).[3] We can differentiate this contrived episode from past experience and logically predict a second experience.

The investigative subjectivity noticed in this case is relatively useless and weightless unless someone uses his mind to discern and interpret the useful information from the unsaturated evidence for the ears of a jury. Such information by its very nature must be couched in degrees proportional to the integrity seen in the evidence. Intuitive probability is a power for action used to express a passionate concern for a logical, reasonable answer; a passionate conviction arising from a rudimentary hint, a disquieting reality, a just and necessary inference that rationally backfills the empty categories existing in the event. Subjective probability, rather than an obstacle, becomes a means of mutual communication, an exchange medium for productive dialogue that allows an interdisciplinary translation to occur for jury consideration. Such statements to a jury are graduated, credible, representational responses

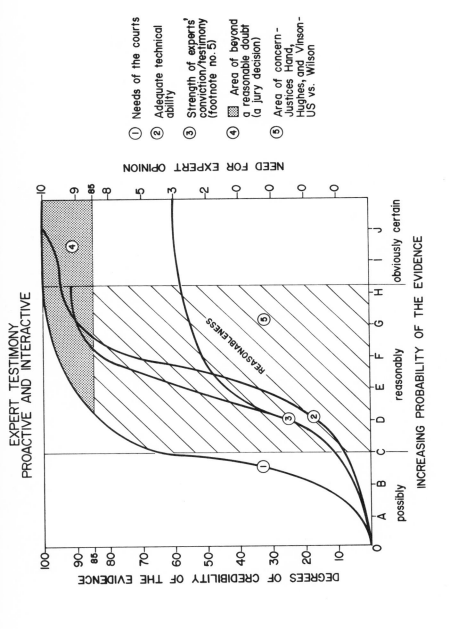

EXPERT TESTIMONY
PROACTIVE AND INTERACTIVE

NEED FOR EXPERT OPINION

DEGREES OF CREDIBILITY OF THE EVIDENCE

INCREASING PROBABILITY OF THE EVIDENCE

possibly reasonably obviously certain

REASONABLENESS

① Needs of the courts

② Adequate technical
   ability

③ Strength of experts'
   conviction/testimony
   (footnote no.5)

④ Area of beyond
   a reasonable doubt
   (a jury decision)

⑤ Area of concern -
   Justices Hand,
   Hughes, and Vinson -
   US vs. Wilson

to serve the truth; this truth statement in reality is but a synthesis of the meaningful coordinates that can exist in the imperfect evidence and when seen, it must be expressed in order to increase the limits of belief for each juror and to bring justice to the victims. This is not chance, not an accident, but an anomaly, a happy event in the inherent natural order seen in these current events. This observed order is not at all strange to our everyday experience of knowing that which is normal. These flexible statements allow for consideration of individual circumstances in each case and are a recognition that every crime scene is a multifaceted and a multilevel reality that requires distinct individual actions. We have lost all perspective if we permit contrived appearances to hide this reality. Only inductive reasoning will reveal the thin veneer covering the issues and the deliberate perversions, the contrived appearances hiding this reality.

Over the years in the criminal justice system, there has developed a disparity between the needs of the victims of criminal violence as expressed in this book and the philosophy and basic orientation currently expressed in modern, no risk, crime laboratory case reporting. Those who have not yet actively participated in the suggested process seem not to be programmed for appropriate responsiveness due to a lack of training, discernment, insulation, and/or present administrative C.Y.A. safety policies, which avoids responsibility by avoiding any decision that is less than certain. This avoidance of accountability is invisible to the public and to high police officials. It is nevertheless a story of dismal failure in government. These analysts have not been given the proper flexibility, encouragement, nor the mandate to exercise their expertise in so many of these obvious criminal cases. If more acceptance were placed on allowing these subordinates to make their mistakes early and often in their careers, on the more minor cases, each case experience could cumulatively become a constructive, compassionate approach to problem solving as they increase in knowledge, experience, and seniority. This attitude to become involved could mature, and many more multiples of the more serious police cases would have their day in court and not be lost from jury review. The present, crucial prosecutorial vulnerability and impotency could be overcome through the efforts of a concerned expert who recognizes that identifiable random events do occur in a predictable matrix in most criminal cases. In the eyes of any truthful, critical observer, for too many years and in too many instances the criminal justice system (CJS) has been trying to open a complicated lock with the wrong key. Since there are very strong self-serving policies in place, very few police managers even consider the possibility that we might be using the wrong keys, let alone to begin to look for the proper ones!

If such an admission is ever made, perhaps then it will be seen that our crime laboratory reports have been as inadequate as green tea in most cases and that this would not have occurred had there been sunset legislation in place, an oversight surveillance committee or the equivalent of a government accounting office (GAO) to insure the effectiveness of these laboratories and of the specific experts employed in them. Presently there is no account-ability for the severe miscarriages of justice now prevalent in many of these organizations.[4] Since there are few pressures on these experts to perform to any predetermined standard of effec-tiveness, the criminal cases not brought to trial now quietly fall conveniently between bureaucratic cracks and are lost forever from view.

These oversight committees will be needed until the profes-sion is swamped with analysts who not only say "yes" to the suggested or similar proposition, but who actually grasp the pre-dictability theme and consciously respond. The new analysts will then realize that this is a beginning and nothing else will do; there is no other substitute for the feeling of being really connected, really involved with life and with the victims in their misery and pain.

To correct the misdirection, a different orientation has to be accepted. All analysts will at last have to admit that all their scientific decisions are only tentative and that all criminal cases submitted to court must be couched in some form of analytical, subjective probability—none of which will ever reach unity or certainty—and this does create controversy and risk for them when testifying in a court of law.

With the above foremost in mind and with the vivid understanding that every crime laboratory, due to unalterable case circumstances, is a strong state monopoly, such units need not be efficient but must be effective in meeting the needs of the victims of criminal violence. This is especially so since the victims of criminal violence who appeal for assistance have no other choice but to submit to these locally established governmental agencies. In order to document this mandatory effectiveness a managerial tool can be established by developing an Operational Effectiveness Quotient (OE factor) for any crime laboratory or sub-unit of the laboratory that can be used for inter-or intralaboratory comparisons. Each crime laboratory produces enormous case statistics in the annual reports, i.e. the number of cases submitted for analysis, the numbers of items handled, the number of tests performed, et cetera. The OE factor can reflect a more meaningful effectiveness factor than heretofore available, for the laboratories themselves, their sub-units, and the individual experts as well as for the police and general public who pay for these services.

T_c = total number of criminal cases submitted to crime laboratory or any sub-unit

T_i = total number of cases submitted to court in the I-J category—obviously certain

A_p = applied (subjective) probabilities E‑H category—cases less than certain submitted for court review

$$OE = \frac{Tc}{Ap} \qquad \text{or} \qquad OE = \frac{Tc - Ti}{Ap}$$

= Public Accountability and Social Responsibility to the Victims of Violent Crimes = Achievement Factor

The nearer this stewardship/surveillance quotient (OE factor) comes to unity, the more each category being measured is meeting the needs of the victims, society, and of the courts by rendering more substantive due process than was previously available. It is very similar to a low ERA (earned run average) in baseball that quantifies a pitcher's performance between his peers and those in all other baseball clubs and leagues. The lower the ERA the more effective any particular pitcher is in the game. It is thought (guess estimate with a high confidence factor of being correct) that the national average for crime laboratory experts handling criminal cases is far above an OE factor (ERA) of one thousand + (vs. 1.2 or 1.3) reflecting that only the cases deemed to be certain ever leave the laboratory for jury consideration. (What professional pitcher would be allowed to pitch and have an ERA equal to one thousand or anything close to it?) Furthermore, if the OE factor ratio + / − is less than 6:1, reflecting an unacceptable level of negative conclusions being drawn from the submitted case evidence (garbage in—garbage out syndrome), there will be a strong need to more severely monitor the quality control features on all incoming laboratory case submissions because there is now no excuse to be so indifferent to the victims of violent crimes.

The OE factor is a technical as well as an administrative device that raises the demand for more information in the submitted reports going to court by forcing the analyst to be more sensitive to the disembodied but compatible circumstantial evidence that is available. It will objectively indicate how the experts are responding or not responding to crime scene reality and adapting to the victims' needs. The OE factor calls those entrusted with a serious responsibility to account, since that which is given in trust demands responsible actions. The master program followed so closely in the past will be forced to change and reflect a more ethical concern for the victims in their written reports and this reestablishes a moral symmetery for the victims of criminal violence. To maintain a low OE factor demands a more influential analyst for disseminating the available information to a jury. The OE factor, if used as an antidote to the present master program, will force a confrontation with reality and force a new process of decision making for the benefit of the victims, since it demands that the residual injustices now present in so many criminal cases be noticed. Any criminal court expert exposed to this review is one whose ratio of values and past conditioning will have had to change from that of the present style, that of only being a spoon-feed, quality control chemist with the associated timid case reporting, to an authentic criminalist producing creative cases analyses. This is mandatory because the courts are information intensive and this strategy will more effectively satisfy this need.

When a criminal case is not properly analyzed, when the unlocking realization or disquiet reality is overlooked (the imperfect evidence is suppressed), no alarms go off, no bells ring, no pain is felt, no one balks, no one in the laboratory gets excited, no investigation is made, no other person questions the ignored reality. All is calm, quiet, and passive as the case gets a wave off. There are no systems analysts in the nation's crime laboratories due to the uniqueness of each case. Each worker is technically unsupervised with few case quality controls in place at any time due to the complexities of most criminal cases. The victims can be dealt a hand from the bottom of the deck and no one objects. Since all of the above is true, there has obviously been serious and prolonged abdication of managerial responsibility to maintain proper surveillance controls within each affected crime laboratory or specific discipline, and therefore the number of victims violated twice nationally must be staggering. The salient point is the need for the establishment of the OE factor high in the administrative structure to monitor the procedures and quickly identify inappropriate activities in these crime laboratories. These working analysts are necessary for society to function but their present extreme autonomy is not appreciated. The OE factor, if used as a reset button, will eliminate the rigid procedures, the timid reports that deform the process of justice, and remake the present controlling dynasties. It will be an indicator of effective resistance to the marauders of society. The present procedural limitations must not be allowed to continue to be at war with veracity. What is required is a clear device that has meaning for nontechnical senior police management to restore their own and the public's confidence in heretofore unmonitored public service organizations. If a piano player is the sole expert in deciding if the piano is in tune, it will never be otherwise. This is not permitted in music; it cannot be permitted in criminalistics. What is needed is tangible action rather than more examples of missed opportunities and excuses if we are to prevent similar episodes from continuing to happen. We cannot let the system monitor itself as it has been because without adequate follow-up measures and surprise inspections to assure compliance to the victim's needs (maintaining a low OE factor), the passivity will continue and the real issues sidestepped and otherwise avoided simply due to tradition. It is a well-known managerial principle that the working analysts are most interested in and do what is inspected—not what you expect. The introduction of these measures is an effort to preserve the system from its own errors; to discipline the system, to reform it but not to fundamentally destroy it. Any objection to these inspections or to the use of inductive probability in the vast majority of criminal cases, is but to flout our public commitment to these victims of criminal violence.

One significant advantage that the present system has had that has prevented this inquiry from having surfaced long ago in the past was that no one has kept any statistics on the effectiveness of the crime laboratories vis-a-vis the number of cases processed and their individual impact in the courts. Perhaps such a system of monitoring performance was never developed because no one wanted to know the size of the problem or advertise to the police, public or the courts the number of victims of violent crimes who are being violated a second time due to our aversion to meet our responsibilities. It might have been seen as a self-fulfilling prophecy of doom if the general public became aware of how ineffective crime laboratories actually have been in assisting the police to meet their responsibilities.[5] Our prolonged inability to renounce these failures of being so immune from all frictions with reality has to be staggering to any detached and prudent observer of the scene. With chilling clarity it becomes all too apparent that being so technically paranoid (isomers and analogs zero error, et cetera) has materially contributed to the 50:1 ratio of reported crimes to convictions now present in our national crime statistics. To continue to accept this ratio for 5.5 million victims each year is sheer official duplicity, an effrontery to the victims of criminal violence.

With the above observations of this social tragedy, how can we professional criminalists ignore or justify nonuse of the suggested scheme and maintain any credibility as criminal court prosecution experts? If we fail to meet this challenge we will remain hypocritical court experts who are technically irrelevant (experts by default) since we are more concerned with our own professional survival than to be of service to the courts or to our fellow human beings who are the victims of circumstance, sometimes so vile as to be beyond imagination.

MEANINGFUL DISCLOSURES

1. It is anticipated that there can be a similarity drawn between the objective scale that describes the frequency, the estimated strength, and magnitude of an earthquake occurring many hundreds of miles away to the individual jurors' subjective accumulative belief in the guilt or innocence of the defendant at trial. The former registers in an increasing graduated, progressive logarithmic series, in numerical notations the size of the eruption; the latter does the exact same mentally. See Chapter Four and its footnote #4 for similarity to the synapse theory.

2. This system of justice places a great weight on the prosecution and on the victim to prove his case at trial. If any one of us were to be unjustly accused at any future trial, we would readily appreciate this advocatory system of justice and realize that it should not be any other way. This text pleads that the victim should have an equally strong defense by the prosecution team. Such effort has to be shared responsibility (with the victim) on the part of the police, the crime laboratory, and the prosecuting attorney so that a comprehensive case can be given to a trial jury more often.

3. Can one consider oneself an authentic expert to guide an expedition for an elephant hunt, if after a three day journey, the "expert" cannot tell his novice clients that elephants are near until they are actually heard and then seen by all—the animals romping in tall grass with the associated noise and widespread damage to the high grass that any of these amateurs can clearly see themselves? If on the previous day's journey, if large animal tracks were noticed and trees were seen to have been damaged with their tree barks torn off, would it not have been possible to have estimated the presence of and the time lapse from when the elephants did damage to the trunks of trees or to feel the heat or absence of same in elephant droppings found on the trail among the tracks, so as to estimate the time lapse and numbers of animals

present in the herd? To have missed these preliminaries and to have no better "hearing" or insight than his clients until the very last hours of the journey certainly disqualifies this individual as any kind of an expert elephant guide.

Finding a person with a smoking gun in their hand, standing over a dead person who has been shot demands a good explanation on the part of the sole witness. In the absence of an explanation there is a high probability of that person being the killer. It is not necessary to have seen the fired bullets actually enter the body and see the deceased fall with the associated loss of body fluids before reasonable conclusions can be drawn, explanations weighed, and decisions made. The law of substraction is an important consideration for any jury consideration at this point.

4. The absence of any governing regulation or surveillance device permits unregulated freedom of analysis and the toll for this oversight for the victims of criminal violence has to be unconscionably high in any jurisdiction that places a high regard on faultless and riskless examinations! A worthwhile enhancement for the victims of criminal violence would be to substitute the suggested OE factor as a new primary reinforcement catalyst; then past programmed professional conditioning (being a systematic theorist) will be given a new goal to become more adaptable to change, introspection and inference through behavior modification (Pavlov's dogs, Thorndike's cats, Skinner's rats). If new rewards, punishments and repetitions are considered, these adjustments will change behavioral attitudes, cognitive processes, and problem-solving techniques to better cope with circumstances that are so highly situational! The expert for the prosection will then be the interface or the connecting link he is supposed to be, between the true reality of a crime scene and the jury's critical need to be appropriately informed. No longer will the expert's perception of the obvious be considered remarkable or uncanny (reconsider the above footnote #3).

5. This text has concentrated on the performance of crime laboratories but these units are not the only areas within the criminal justice system that are delinquent to the needs of the victims of criminal violence.

Chapter 13

A SHAM

But there is really no scientific or other method by which man can steer safely between the opposite dangers of believing too little or too much. To face such dangers is apparently our duty and to hit the right channel between them is a measure of our wisdom as men. What should be preached is courage weighed with responsibility.

—William James

Anyone who indicates that there is a fixed response to these problem cases doesn't understand the problems because the target (case solutions) keeps moving. What is needed is critical, independent thinking.

—Robert C. Sullivan

The contents of this volume depict the personal experiences of the author as he matured in a specialized field of law enforcement known as criminalistics. Due to what is now viewed as many serendipitous events, the author's career goals and concerns forced him to critically review his professional experiences. When he became more alert to the technical voids that existed in so many cases and of the frustrations subjectively accumulating in him for many years, he attempted to construct a viable decision matrix that would quiet these concerns of conscience. For too many years he had been as guilty as any and perhaps more guilty than most for not even attempting to solve these problems in crime laboratory decision making sooner. These accounts document his evolution and the suggested solutions to these problems that have for too long gone unnoticed by the general public. His obligations to these victims of criminal violence and to his profession to overcome these absurd violations in logic are now almost finished. Much time had been wasted in his unquestioning loyalty to his profession until a supreme event forced him to deny that loyalty for another, higher loyalty, to the idea of justice for the victims who are not being heard and concern for the resulting miscarriages of justice in these same cases. He was aware from personal experiences that the victims were being denied their democratic heritage since too often there was justice for the criminals and a travesty in justice for the victims. If there be any debt owing vis-à-vis the victims he ignored prior to the development of this decision format, in 1975–79, hopefully a more equitable and reciprocal balance at last has now been established. One final set of concerns remains to be accomplished before he lays his pen down.

It has been almost twelve years of intermittent effort to solve and overcome this professional dilemma. Unless these words are turned into action, unless there develops a huge public outcry and concern against the current, terribly confused roles and demonstrated voids in the present reporting efforts from the nation's crime laboratories, all the time and effort will have been in vain. The author knows and is all too aware:

• that the worn out cliches of "If it works, don't fix it"; "A negative report is easier to justify and to write than a positive one"; "To get along, you go along"; "Smart people don't ever get involved"; "Maintain zero error in all things administratively as well as technically"; "Prove all cases beyond a scientific doubt"; "Do as little as possible as often as possible"—all done in order to keep a low profile and be as uninvolved as often as possible—will continue to be used as a means of avoiding present reality and our managerial and analytical responsibilities in all future criminal cases. These are deep-seated defensive mechanisms of long standing to avoid the uncomfortable and incomplete truth present in almost all criminal cases. They appear to some to be terribly, terribly sweet except that they conceal hidden agendas of noninvolvement in the more difficult cases. They all aid the self-serving power elite to successfully avoid their commitment to society and to the victims of criminal violence.

• that without honest indignation at the injustices so often seen in the evidence, without the process recording of our experiences by the individual analyst and redirecting the inner rhythm that now fails to see the overwhelming cogency (relevance), the strategic connections in the evidence in each case, no gestalt closure (the expression of the justified inference) will be anticipated, attempted, or recognized. No use of subjective probability will be mandated or even thought to be justified and no expression of professional convictions will be permitted. We will continue to be "rule bound" with no sympathetic understanding of the latent, burning reality. The need for the meticulous recording of technical minutiae will continue to be overpowering. We will continue to suppress the truth even as we search for it because we refuse to rethink tradition. The gross miscarriages of justice will continue to go unnoticed because the flawed perfections inevitably present in almost all criminal cases—the voids—will not be permitted to be overcome. Such counsel from police superiors for these chemists "to toe the line," and "to stay within prescribed lines" has the force of law upon subordinates who depend on these superiors for their professional survival and their promotions.

• that the disquiet realities in so many cases will be ignored because there are presently neither internal incentives nor external competition to be effective (since a severe monopoly does exist) and alert to the many less than perfect cases and their unspoken, tight connections that can be crucial in many hundreds of investigations. The fact that a developed conscience must be the final guide to actions is never considered.

• that there will be a hue and cry from many analysts who will, in rebuttal, protest that it can't be done for any number of valid technical reasons. These negative, ostrich-like individuals will conveniently overlook the many instances where it has been done. The lessons learned from Locard, Fleming, Paul Stombaugh, Milton Halpern, and George Conova are grudgingly acknowledged only as isolated events. They forget that in determined and willing hands the tight associations, the educated projections in criminal cases are as apparent as were those visible sneaker impressions quietly leading those who will but follow, literally, to the perpetrator's bedroom door. Only when such evidence is presented to the triers of fact can the conscience of the community be expressed and the conscience of the authentic criminalist be put to rest. Only when such evidence is presented to the triers of fact can the community's conscience be expressed. To continue on the present, well-worn path is an outrage to these victims and their loved ones.

• The function of this faith projection in the natural order and the subsequent use of subjective probability is not to reduce the mystery to a rational clarity but to integrate the irresistible combinations seen in the evidence, with the known, together, into a living whole. Using inductive probability is an adaptive response to reality. The examiner is then able to appropriately transcend the limitations of the incomplete (secondary) circumstantial evidence. This will create a bursting blatter of new information for jury consideration. This is the only way of opening up the true depths of the reality present in so many of these otherwise rejected cases.

• Defense attorneys, whose presence is guaranteed to all defendants in criminal trials under *Gideon vs. Wainwright* 372 US335 (1963) in fulfilling their proper obligations to the accused at trial, will clamor in vigorous protest about the "injustice" heaped upon their clients by the mere reasonableness and cumulativeness of the prosecution's "circumstantial" evidence. To justify their subsequent evasive actions, a flimsy philosophy has developed among most defense attorneys that their clients need not really be innocent of the crime charged, but just be judged one way or another not guilty in court by a panel of his peers. To this end there will be almost endless postponements and continuances requested prior to trial, used as delaying tactics in an attempt to discourage any witnesses and especially the victim; if this fails, the defense will harass the prosecutor's witnesses, expert and otherwise at trial (their appearance for cross-examination by the defense guaranteed under *Washington vs. Halman* 245 F Supp116 MD ala 1965) in an attempt to minimize their testimonies. They will demand that the civil rights of the accused be observed by taking full advantage of the Fifth Amendment (a good law), their rights of discovery, the exclusionary rule (evidence suppression under *Mapp vs. Ohio* 367 US 643 [1961]—a poor law that was slightly revised in 1968 to allow "stop and frisk" measures in justified instances), any minor defect in the chain of evidence custody or rules of trial procedure; in any search and seizure warrants, any Miranda or Escobedo slips and then, of course, plea bargaining will be attempted. They will attempt to put the victim on trial and if possible, will attempt to make the victim responsible for his own murder. They will demand every test imaginable in order to skirt or confuse the main issue and all with no regard for basic morality, logic, or justice for the victim. After the trial and the required unanimous guilty verdict, there will of course be efforts for sentence reductions, probation, and endless appeals based on the numerous and zealous objections registered during the trial exactly for that purpose—to establish the need for the appeal. Such objections to procedure are a typical lawyer's cunning response to technicalities for their own sake in defense of their clients. At no time is there any thought for the basic civil rights of the victim, or any thought to the need for retribution for the crimes committed. They have learned to use the delicate legal system to their advantage. The prosecution of these cases must do likewise but only an equally aggressive prosecution using proactive experts can counter and readjust this serious imbalance. To withhold similar aggressive support from the victims is to render inequitable treatment to the innocent majority when they become subjects of a crime of violence. The author is also aware that the many negative processes used to destroy his professional career, to punish his impertinence of daring to constructively criticize his professional peers in these matters are firmly established and grudgingly peers in those he has left behind. The touchstone of the matter is that if public institutions are permitted to ruthlessly silence and surpass these compassionate, analytical concerns for the victims of violent crimes, the situation will never be solved since the system is not open to the thoughtful change and any dissent from concerned experts becomes treason. Any challenge to present policy or orthodoxy is met with instant punitive action on those who have a conscience and/or who have the guts of their convictions.

These repressive measures are delivered without regard to written admininstrative or departmental policies, the analyst's responsibilities to the courts, constitutional guarantees, or the jury's need to know. These realities are as real as they are terrible! Somehow, whistleblowers, ethical resistors who have a conscience and whose guilt, compassion, or reponsibilities have been stirred, have to be protected from bureacrats who foster a constant policy of C.Y.A. rather than meeting their professional obligations to these victims. To this day the Caesars always kill the messengers who bring the bad news to them. We are utterly naive if we believe that these artificially contrived circumstances and hidden agendas have failed to send a strong negative message to all who would harbor similar thoughts to aggressively aid other victims of criminal violence as a proactive, interactive prosecution's expert witness. Their reservoirs for combativeness have been effectively neutralized. This malpractice is only superceded by the industrywide silence known to exist in the professional ranks. Such silence is the accepted alternative to avoid controversy, peer rejection, professional and personal isolation, or worse. If these institutions were functioning in the private sector more effective methods would have been devised long ago to reduce the 50:1 ratio that plagues society today.

• There is no present method to guarantee that if the decision voids are now adequately filled, this suggested solution will be anything but a temporary and an isolated incident. The suggested program was difficult and obviously time-consuming to develop, and it will be even more difficult to promote and implement since there is no meaningful pressure on these organizations to alter their present, well-established, comfortable, structured procedures. We are dealing with a suffocating, self-protecting bureaucratic monopoly with ingrained resistance to change because they are creatures of inertia. The scientific traditions do not address themselves to the needs of the victims of violent crimes. The OE factor will force a behavioral and attitudinal change in the system to society's benefit because the criminal trial juries can now be alerted to the fact that there is a very high degree of predisposition and predictability in the incomplete criminal evidence found at most crime scenes.

There is an educated incapacity to be inductive (viewed as being occupationally disabled since emphasis is on fact acquisition and memorization versus problem-based learning) or to realize the second order effects of their (non) actions. These experts fail to realize that most criminal cases coming into a crime laboratory are not conducive to static test applications. There is no emphasis that there is a very high degree of predisposition and predictability in most criminal cases, that the examiners' observations are individually compelling except with regards to the technically perfect cases (I-J).

All of the above must not be allowed to continue if this creeping disaster in the criminal justice system is to be stopped, if society is to have any chance of surviving. We, as citizens of a dynamic nation, have the means to make our concerns known at the highest levels of federal, state, and local governments. These are the agencies that can translate public sentiment into political power. Unless individual state legislatures are moved to correct these injustices and establish at least an equivalent to the suggested OE factor, the well-entrenched bureacrats will not change. The victims of violent crimes will continue to be violated by the very system that has been established for society's protection and to which these citizens have given financial support through their own state and local taxes. A successful campaign for large-scale repair and reconstruction of the basic infrastructure of scientific law enforcement must be undertaken by those most affected by it. The status quo must be disrupted and repaired.

If we permit this devastating mockery of justice to continue, then society will give a clear signal to and will deserve the Ted Bundys, the Richard Specks and the Harold Klines in our midst. We will have learned nothing from the tragedy visited upon the Alday family and it all will be allowed to be repeated again and again since our past behavior of doing nothing does not bode well for a better future. Ted Bundy is thought to have killed over thirty women—thirty rebuffs to Locard, Fleming, and Dr. Halpern. From the Northwest in the mid-seventies to Florida in 1980, where he has continued to make a mockery of our criminal system for at least the last eight years while on death row,[1] Richard Speck ruthlessly and without hesitation or compassion killed eight nurses in their dormitory and escaped the death penalty. He will have the gall to petition the state for a parole in a few months' time. Harold Kline was a neighbor of Kitty Genovese in Queens, New York. According to former New York City Chief of Detectives Albert Seedman, Kline actually saw the killer of Kitty Genovese, Winston Moseley, in his final attack upon this neighbor in the hallway of his own apartment house and did nothing to assist her—not even a phone call to the police. He saw the situation; he knew something terrible was happening and he ignored his responsibilities to another needful human being. This was a cold, irresistibly repugnant reaction to this situation and to his innate responsibilities to this unfortunate and desperate human being.[2]

The Alday family—father, uncle, three sons, and daughter-in-law—was found slaughtered in a trailer home located in one of the Southern states. Each had been shot in the back of the head as the result of an apparent robbery. The four defendants, when arrested the next day at a distant location, pleaded guilty not only to the police, but to TV and the print media shortly after their arrests and again in open court during their trial. At the trial they were found guilty by a jury of their peers and sentenced to death. It has taken ten years to appeal these convictions on the basis that the trial judge did not grant "a change of venue" when requested by the defense attorney although, throughout the entire ten year period of time (trial and appeals), the confessions were never recanted by any one of the defendants. This was a procedural dispute—not a material challenge to the facts in the case. Based on what is considered again to be arid, repugnant, perverted legalism, the convictions were overturned by a three-judge federal court of appeals and remanded back to the lower trial court for a new trial. (Hopefully, this defense ploy will not ultimately succeed due to the confessions originally obtained and now on the record.)[3] Once again, the ethical truth was denied because process overcame good common sense, inductive reasoning, morality, leadership, and compassion for the victims of these criminal acts. In a nutshell, the present criminal justice system is a *failed monopoly* in which the victims of criminal violence have had no controls and little appeal.

The brutality of these collective attacks on justice is almost limitless and eclipsed only by the apathy of Kitty Genovese's neighbors and of the unconcerned analysts mentioned in these pages, who see their responsibilities and view the incomplete evidence and do nothing to correct the situation. They are guilty bystanders, all. There is something terribly wrong in all of these negative cases if society has any compassion at all for the victims of criminal violence or any basic conception of justice. We are in a midst of a self-reinforcing disaster and this failed monopoly must be corrected.[4]

Notice has been given to other killers to leave no witnesses to their crimes with the almost certain expectation that the incomplete (secondary) circumstantial evidence inevitably left behind by these culprits will be left untouched by most technical investigators since they will not violate established ineffective policies regardless of the circumstances. Crimes will tend to become more numerous and more violent. Our systematic lack of personal involvement (internalization) with the incomplete evidence gives full acknowledgment to our ignoring the needs of these victims. The agenda now being followed is absolutely wrong and it must be corrected if we wish to eliminate these episodic horrors.

To deny the victims of violent crime the assistance they require is nothing less than criminal—for you and for me as a criminalist. The Good Samaritan of biblical fame did stop to give meaningful assistance to a fellow human being in time of need because he had compassion for the stranger, he had the opportunity to do so and most importantly the social, human responsibility to respond even though it did cost him material inconvenience. We too must penetrate the moral apathy and overcome the fundamental contradiction now so prevalent in this society and allow ourselves to become prisoners of conscience. Otherwise we cease to be advocates for these helpless victims.

Dear reader, give some serious thought to the real possibility of what would have happened to the victim had the Good Samaritan never stopped. The victim would have been in desperate peril had the Good Samaritan ignored his responsibilities as his peers had done. They practiced secular humanism. The Good Samaritan saw, he understood, and acted upon Christian humanism[5] to complete his obligation to his fellow man. It is now time for you to express your acknowledgment of your obligations to these victims of violent crimes as was done in the biblical account so long ago. If you do nothing concerning these issues, it is because you or a loved one have not become a victim and the crime statistics are against you from remaining so uninvolved for too long. Since there are really only two types of citizens—victims and future victims—you too can personally experience the unwitting sham that has developed and is now awaiting you or a member of your household. Haven't you, like myself, been a guilty bystander long enough? I tried to respond many times in recent years and the effort cost me a career of twenty four years. (They again shot the messenger who brought them bad news.) For you to become involved will cost you a postage stamp! If your choice is to remain aloof and uninvolved, a decision will have been made. It will be a passive decision to keep the present outrageous system functioning as it is now. There are many victims who would vote against that option had they known these facts in time. If no action is taken to overcome the cold detachments as seen in these nonaggressive, intrinsically disordered, unbelievably silent reports that document an endless and dismal series of missed opportunities and disasters, then there has been no learning or understanding from this text and the true cases contained herein. Any learning gained demands action on your part. Such understanding of the present dangers will override normal complacency and help reestablish legitimate contact with reality.

Only your concentrated and coordinated help will convert what appears to be the end of this book into what may really be the beginning of a new beginning. It is a rational and a humane mission to accept and use the calculated form of relevant change that has been developed in these pages; it is also rational and humane to have by now developed "a noble anger" concerning how these and so many other true criminal cases are being processed in the nation's crime laboratories. The total human suffering that could be otherwise avoided if matters were different is beyond calculation!

MEANINGFUL DISCLOSURES

1. No mention is made of the countless unsolved crimes nationwide and their "elusive" solutions—the Green River Killings, where in a four-year period at least thirty-four (and counting) lives have been taken with only a small amount of meaningful laboratory input.

2. This is the root injustice in all of these cases. To see the need and refuse to reach out and give some assistance, assistance that only we can give. The "Toy Gun Episode" haunts us all. See Chapter Seven and its footnote #8.

3. In several other similar criminal cases many years had also passed between the initial trial and the successful appeal which also reversed the guilty verdicts and the appeals courts directed that new trials were warranted. The state was then expected to retry the accused on the same evidence even though the witnesses and experts would have in the interim moved, died, or forgotten vivid, essential details, the lack of which the defense attorney then aggressively took full advantage of during the retrial. Then another game of wits begins to the great disadvantage to the original victims who by this time have waited years "for justice." The prosecution, *if the case is ever retried*, will be at a great disadvantage and only be able to develop a weak case, ten years after the fact with a high probability of receiving a "not guilty" jury verdict in the case "due to a lack of sufficient evidence" necessary to convenience this new jury. There is of course, no victim appeal process after a "Not Guilty" jury verdict. The above are additional reasons (if there could possibly be a need for even more reasons) for development of as strong a prosecution case as possible in the first instance.

4. See above footnote and Chapter Six and its footnote #5.

5. The term is to denote a person who accepts moral responsibilities to the victim that are far broader than any narrow, precise, written legal obligation. (It also encompasses that to be a good

Christian one must first understand what it means to be a good Jew! Both religious views place high values on true justice, personal responsibility, pervasive caring and moral stamina.) Christian humanism rejects the "Toy Gun Episode" and all of its negative ramifications and with the same force it absolutely demands appropriate ethical actions regardless of the personal consequences. If this is not acceptable and secular humanism is to prevail, then the only honest alternative would force the removal of the motto "In God We Trust" from our national currency, from the walls of our nation's courtrooms, from our nation's Pledge of Allegiance, and from the oaths of office so often approved and accepted throughout the nation! To ignore or reject Christian humanism and not remove the motto from these public announcements of our fidelity to a higher tenet, produces an absolutely hypocritical situation for everyone!

Secular humanism is an atheistic approach to human relations that accepts only "The Law" as precisely written by other human beings. That which is not prohibited by the written law is acceptable with no other obligations to his fellow man than to obey "The Law." There was no Law to encumber those who saw, ignored, and passed the biblical victim; there was no Law that demanded assistance be given to Kitty Genovese when her need was so obvious (not even a phone call to gain assistance) and there is no Law demanding that the criminal justice system bring justice directly to the victims of criminal violence. Collectively, these onlookers see little or no value in these matters not circumscribed by "The Law." Those who adhere to this school of thought most probably don't appreciate the difference between the Nuremberg Principle and the Nuremberg Defense. (See Chapter Six and its footnote #4 and Chapter Eight and its footnote #2.)

Chapter 14

EPILOGUE

With youth and illusions gone, we must be mentally faithful to ourselves. There can be no inconsistencies between a man's convictions, his conscience, his conduct and his vote.

—Daniel Webster

To appear to be just and yet truly unjust is the highest reach of injustice.

—Plato's Republic

Robert C. Sullivan was an experienced criminalist with over twenty-four years of experience in the field of criminalistics. He has a bachelor's degree in Science (B.S.) from Iona College, New Rochelle, New York, and two master's degrees; Master's in Public Administration (M.P.A.) from the Graduate School of the City College of New York and a Master's Degree in Science (M.S.) from the Graduate School of John Jay College of Criminal Justice, New York. He has given testimony, written and oral, in several thousand criminal cases ranging from assault and burglary cases through vehicle accident and extortion cases to homicide and narcotics cases. He has been accepted as an expert in courts of record in each and every case and in three different states. He has published sixteen technical articles in professional journals and is an author of a text book in the field of criminalistics entitled, *Criminalistics—Theory & Practice*, published by Ally & Bacon, 1970. It remains in publication for over sixteen years and has been used in over one hundred colleges in the United States.

He is a member and a fellow of the professional association, the American Academy of Forensic Science, since 1970.

Mr. Sullivan has been associated with three crime laboratories in his career and his expertise has been documented and awarded each time, as he received supervisory and management promotions with each new assignment as his career advanced. He was Senior Technical Supervisor, New York City Crime Laboratory, where he worked for sixteen years. While employed there he received four commendations for excellent work performances. Upon his retirement from the New York City Crime Laboratory, he was selected to be the first Chief Criminalist of the Washington State Crime Laboratory in Seattle, Washington. He remained in this position for over six years and while working in Seattle he received the 1976 Law Enforcement Commendation Medal from the national society's Sons of the American Revolution "in recognition of outstanding achievement." In 1980 he applied for and was appointed to be the first state Director of the Department of Public Safety Crime Laboratory in Flagstaff, Arizona.

He has taught at three Universities with increasing academic rank; lecturer at John Jay College of Criminal Justice in New York City; instructor at the University of Puget Sound in Seattle, Washington; and then adjunct professor at Northern Arizona University, in Flagstaff, Arizona. In accepting the new position in 1980 he was selected by both the Arizona Department of Public Safety (DPS) and Northern Arizona University (NAU) to be, simultaneously, the director of the new crime laboratory in Flagstaff and a member of the academic staff of the University, to materially assist in the establishment of a new academic degree program in criminalistics from the baccalaureate to the Ph.D degree. He concurrently directed the creation of this (on the state campus) new crime laboratory literally from the dirt floor phase to the final acceptance and subsequent full operation of the facility while also teaching at the state university as per his written job description.

Mr. Sullivan was fired from his position as director of the State Crime Laboratory in Flagstaff after thirty months on the pretext of irreconcilable philosophical differences, insubordination, and incompetency on August 20, 1982.[1] In doing so, the state of Arizona, in bureaucratic desperation, used this fictive causality to undermine his credibility and in doing so they violated their own written departmental policies and procedures, equity, and common decency. It was a cut and dried affair because he was an "employee at will."[2] This firing stifled criticism and strengthened the enemies of reform when such reform was imminent and weakened the efforts of those in sympathy with the victims of criminal violence; it gave official protection to the present policy structure and method of analysis as described in these pages.[3] The members of the hearing board would have made poor criminal investigators since no attempt was made to look for a hidden agenda (censorship) that was there.

Mr. Sullivan had again taken a stand for victim advocacy by submitting to a court of law a less than perfect LSD case. The report that was submitted to court stated that "there was a very high probability that LSD was present" in the case. This testimony was both honest and true, but was denounced (after the fact) by those who were not ready to face the appalling facts even though the evidence to do so was enormous.[4] This approach was not appreciated nor desired by the bureaucracy and he, as the senior analyst, was forced to withdraw the submitted positive written court report and reissue a negative report to the same court of record, a report that he, as the expert analyst in the case, did not agree with.[5] The professional opinions he had at last developed, while in Seattle, were in the process of being published in a professional journal and these violated the organizational demands for doctrinal loyalty and conformity regardless of the emphatic insight developed in the criminal evidence. These opinions would not be tolerated by the establishment in Arizona regardless of the moral or academic principles involved. During this period of time, in conclusion to research efforts begun years before on the

211

same subject, a second technical paper was in the process of being published under the auspices of the state university. In March 1982, the powers that be reviewed the preliminary document, after which he was told to withdraw his second (of three) papers from publication as they had the LSD report two months before. When he refused this time on professional, academic, and moral grounds, his superiors told him that "We will do all in our power to stop that publication."[6] They did not succeed in squelching the second of three papers for it was published over their objections in October 1982 in the *Journal of Police Science and Administration*. (The first paper of the series appeared in the same professional journal in June of 1980). However, Mr. Sullivan was punished (prior restraint?) using these phantom issues and paid the price with his career for that insubordination, three months prior to the publication event and therefore adjudged guilty before the fact—before the offense was even committed. He had to be somehow branded an outcast to prevent this challenge from spreading. He had become a critic of the system and its policies and therefore in the eyes of some, a dangerous commodity and even anti-establishment, despite his long and credible career in law enforcement. The mice had been gored and had to somehow fight back. The police authorities evidently were convinced that the ends do justify the means and so the truth of the situation had to be suppressed because "the powers that be" could not allow a palace revolt to take hold. Such a frame-up is about as vile and low a thing as can be done to a human being or by any human being to another. The entire episode could be viewed as being self-contradictory if the needs of the victims of criminal violence had high priority within the criminal justice system; it isn't and they don't.[7]

The author is still trying to raise the level of public sentiment for these victims of criminal violence because he believes that we all have a collective responsibility to correct the documented failures from within the system.

Will you help in this endeavor?

Will you pick up where Mr. Sullivan has been forced to leave off? We have all been walking around with a ticking, unexploded bomb long enough. If you, dear reader, will not do something to materially correct the situation for these victims of criminal violence, you have not understood (or believed) the contents of this book. To say that you wish something done or changed without trying to gain the power, position, or influence to gain that power to do it, is really tantamount to not wanting it done at all. It is basically a test of wills and only you the citizen, consumer of these services, can be the cordite that can bring this house of cards down and rebuild a more responsive effective bureaucracy. You too must flower where you are planted.

In a similar situation in India, when Mohandas Gandhi was "fighting" against British home rule, he was asked how he could hope to succeed against such an immense world power. He replied that the absolute worst thing to do was to do nothing! "Do something for the cause no matter how small the effort."

Another famous leader, Edmund Burke, once said that "Evil exists in the world only because good people knowing of its existence do nothing about it." Public hope (that things can be made better) can be public folly but only if we allow it to be so, only if we cease to be an apathetic society. If we continue to be so detached from these concerns, we will be a community that does not wish to defend itself and as such we literally will be a society that does not deserve to survive. It is time for this society to let out a primal scream!

Give a damn and don't be another Pontius Pilate![8] Only by doing so can we show real concern for these victims of criminal violence and only then reach the action level of our personal commitment to them.

MEANINGFUL DISCLOSURES

1. If these charges were true, then the managers of three large crime laboratories are equally incompetent for having selected and promoted the author to hold increasingly responsible technical, supervisory, and management positions over a twenty-four year period of time; the administrators and appointing faculty of three universities are equally incompetent for allowing him to be admitted to their staffs, with increasing academic status, to teach forensic science to their students; the trial courts of three states are incompetent for permitting his personal technical testimony in several hundred criminal cases and in accepting his technical written decisions in many thousands of other cases. (The convicted defendants in all of these cases should file writs of habeas corpus because they were convicted and are being denied their freedoms based on incompetent testimony.) The Milton Halperns of the world must also be wrong when they also "see" and try to report to the criminal courts the comprehensible realities in the cases described in these pages; the four justices of the U.S. Supreme Court (Hand, Hughes, Vinson, and Cardoza) must be wrong when they tried to give direction and *correlated* the law to criminal reality and its relationship to human events. Lastly, if we are to be consistent, we must ignore the serendipitous (mysterously arranged) "accidents" described in these pages and accept the present operating theory and self induced value system that only secular humanistic principles can be considered in a court of law; we must accept that the pleas of the Kitty Genoveses of the world can be blamelessly ignored and their cases lost by default; that the uniformed officer in Chapter Seven, footnote #8 was wrong in performing his duty—and that the second officer was correct in following a policy of CYA and that the really smart people never do get involved. If this be the case, then all of us will some day come to realize how ineffective the present criminal justice really is and how isolated and uncared for the present victims of criminal violence really are.

2. This designation in legal terms means that any employee who is not specifically "under contract" has no inherent right to any job in which he is employed. It means that such employees can be fired from their positions "for the right reasons, for a wrong reason, or for no reason at all." Such an employee can be fired "if he changes the side on which he parts his hair" and the employer dislikes the change. This opinion was given to the author by the American Civil Liberties Union in Phoenix, Arizona in June, 1983.

3. From a "professional" point of view something had to be done to silence the new developing theory, otherwise the powers that be would be embarrassed and subjected to criticism for not having developed this tenet long ago and for failing to have brought reparation to so many past victims of criminal violence. How this was to be done far outweighed the consequences of allowing this thesis to mature. Since there was "no (written law" preventing repugnant acts against "an employee-at-will" (what is not prohibited is permitted), the foul act was completed regardless of the violation of ethics involved. A very important supporting factor to consider is that in any nonprofit institution, individual performance is judged by one's peers, not by the consumer of these services. Any ideological deviation from conventional performance or from the status quo, regardless of the motivation for such behavior, is most often fatal to that person's career; it is far more important for the powers that be to discredit any such critic of the system for reasons of self-preservation and control than it is for them to find the truth. In the face of such official and united opposition, peer compliance against the critic (group think) is known to be extraordinarily high.

4. The legitimate leap in logic that this case required is the same as that applied in the M-N-O-P events in Chapter #7 and its footnote #5. The disquiet reality of the situation and ethics demanded that this be done in this case! The Nuremberg Principle lives on. See Chapter Six and its footnote #4.

5. It is supposed to be a crime to harass or intimidate a

criminal court witness and thereby prevent him from testifying in a court of law! This was also a violation of the direction and guidance given to criminal court experts in *U.S. vs. Wilson* (441-F2d, 655, 1971). See Chapter Two and its footnote #2 and Chapter Six and its footnote #1.

6. This negative attitude refuted, among others, the "Curie Principle" which established that scientific research efforts be free, full, and open publications that encourage cross-fertilization of ideas. This unfettered exchange of ideas helps push back the boundaries of knowledge and whether that is a small effort or a large accomplishment is a moot point. It was also a serious effort to institutionalize and enforce present ideology—the unwritten laboratory policy "that all cases must be proven beyond a scientific doubt before they leave the crime laboratory," and that these reports must be within "zero error" parameters, administratively and technically.

7. The experience described is much like being a soldier who is shot in the back while mounted at the parapets, fighting the enemy who are on the outside of the walls. A soldier who has any intelligence realizes that he can be wounded by the enemy if he raises his head above the protective parapet in an effort to defend his country. To be intentionally shot from the rear while doing his duty is difficult to understand. Perhaps the soldier at the parapet had to be eliminated because he was doing the unusual and more correct thing, and if allowed to continue, severe criticisms from army headquarters might be placed on those of his peers and superiors who were not there with him, at the parapets, defending the fort.

In criminalistics, the idea of placing one's head above the parapets as an advocate for the victims of criminal violence is not taught, is not wanted, and those few who try to do so will be dealt with in a very negative fashion.

8. This individual was completely opposite to "the Good Samaritan" in that he too saw an innocent human being in distress,

violated his duty, and did nothing even though it was in his power to do otherwise. He like so many others depicted in these pages, Pontius Pilate would not stand up to the crowds for what he knew was right and over whom he (too) had complete control. The possible political consequences far outweighed the needs of one unsupported, powerless, innocent individual. A Semmelweiss, a Halpern, or a Gandhi he wasn't.

The final question to be answered is: In whose footsteps are we, as individuals, to follow? Is Christian humanism and the Nuremberg Principle meaningful to any of us?

Chapter 15

SOURCES OF APPEAL

All citizens have the right and obligation to petition their respective state senators and representatives on matters of keen concern. These leaders of the community can be specifically identified by calling numerous community oriented organizations, the local library, and county voter registration offices. These individuals should be your primary contacts within your local area.

The following is a partial list of national organizations that should have serious concerns for the victims of violent crimes as a high priority within their organizations. If there is apathy towards the victims of violent crime, it will be quickly changed if these organizations receive thousands of irate letters from determined citizens.

National Association of Attorneys General
Hall of the States
444 North Capital Street
Washington, D.C 20001 (202) 628–0435

Victimology
2333 North Vernon Street
Arlington, Virginia 22207 (703) 528–8872

National Organization for Victim Assistance
717 D Street N.W.
Washington, D.C. 20004 (202) 393–NOVA

International Association of Chiefs of Police
Thirteen Firstfield Road
P.O. Box 6010
Garthersburg, Maryland 20878 (301) 948–0922

American Bar Association
Section on Criminal Justice
1800 M Street 2nd floor
Washington, D.C 20036–5886 (202) 331–2260

National District Attorneys Association
1033 North Fairfax Street, Suite 200
Alexandria, Virginia 22314 (703) 549–9222

Americans for Effective Law Enforcement
5519 North Cumberland Avenue #1008
Chicago, Illinois 60656–1471 (321) 763–2800

National Sheriffs' Association
1450 Duke Street
Alexandria, Virginia 22314 (703) 836–7827

American Law Institute
4025 Chestnut Street
Philadelphia, PA 19104 (215) 243–1600

Citizens' Committee for Victim Assistance
53 West Jackson
Chicago, Illinois 60604 (312) 786–0500

Vera Institute of Justice
30 East 39th Street
New York, New York 10016 (212) 986–6910

Equal Justice Foundation
1346 Connecticut Avenue N.W.
Suite 525
Washington, DC 20036 (202) 452–1267

American Bar Foundation
1155 East 60th Street
Chicago, Illinois 60637 (312) 667–4700

Center for Law in the Public Interest
(095) West Pico Boulevard 3rd floor
Los Angeles, CA 90064–2166 (213) 470–3000

Center for Accountability to the Public
175 East Delaware Place
Chicago, Illinois 60611 (312) 280–7900

National Association of Victims Assistance
1757 Park Road N.W.
Washington, D.C. 20010 (202) 232–8560

American Judicative Society
200 West Monroe Street, Suite 1606
Chicago, Illinois 60606 (312) 558–6900

No one should overlook the interest and power of the local victim rights groups, and newspapers in addition to contacts with the other organizations and state legislators.

BIBLIOGRAPHY

Ayer, A.J., *Probability and Evidence*. New York: Columbia Press, 1972.

Barzun, J. *Science*. New York: Harper and Row Publishers, 1964.

Bolton, Neal. *The Psychology of Thinking*. London: Methuen and Company, Ltd., 1972.

Broudy, H.S. *Truth and Credibility*. New York: Longmon, Inc., 1981.

Bruner, Goodnow, Austin. *A Study of Thinking*. New York: John Wiley & Sons, Inc., 1956.

Carnap, R. *The Logical Concept of Probability*. Chicago: University of Chicago Press, 1962.

Cohen, L.J. *The Implication of Induction*. London: Methuen and Company, 1970.

Cole, Alwyn. *A Search for Certainty and the Uses of Probability*. Private paper, August 27, 1979.

Colodny, Robert. *Beyond the Edge of Certainty*. Englewood Cliffs, New Jersey: Prentice-Hall, Inc., 1975.

Craighead, W.E. *Behavior Modification*. Boston: Houghton-Mifflin, 1981.

DeBono, Edward. *Lateral Thinking*. New York: Harper and Row, 1970.

Griffith, Kathryn. *Judge Learned Hand and the Roll of the Federal Judiciary*. Norman, Oklahoma: University of Oklahoma Press, 1973.

Harrod, Ray. *Foundations of Inductive Logic*. New York: Macmillan, 1974.

James, William. *The Will to Believe*. New York: Dover Publications, 1956.

221

Kelver, H. *The American Jury*. Boston: Little, Brown, 1966.

Kneale, *Probability and Induction*. New York: Oxford University Press, 1949.

May, Rollo. *The Courage to Create*. New York: W.W Norton and Company, Inc., 1975.

Perkins, D.N. *The Mind's Best Work*. Boston: Harvard University Press, 1981.

Polanyi, Michael. *The Tacit Dimension*. New York: Doubleday and Company, Inc., 1966.

Reichenback, Hans. *The Rise of Scientific Philosophy*. Berkeley, California: University of California Press, 1951.

Rescher, Nicholas. *Induction*. Pittsburgh: University of Pittsburgh Press, 1980.

Ruby, Lionel. *The Art of Making Sense*. Philadelphia: J.B. Lippincott Company, 1954.

Scheffler, Israel. *Science and Subjectivity*. Chicago: Bobbs-Merrill Company, Inc., 1967.

Sullivan, R.C., and K.P. O'Brien. "A Systems Approach to Crime Laboratory Management." *Journal of Police Science and Administration,* June 1980, Vol. 8, No. 2, pp. 225–238.

Sullivan, R.C. and R.H. Delaney. "Criminal Investigations: A Decision Making Process." *Journal of Police Science and Administration,* September 1982, Vol. 10, No. 3, pp. 335–343.

Taylor, Irving. *Perspectives in Creativity*. Chicago: Aldine Publishing Company, 1975.

Thornton, John. "Criminalistics—Past, Present and Future." *Lex et Scientia,* Jan–April 1975, Vol. 2, p. 35.

Underwood, Godfrey, ed. *Aspects of Consciousness*. New York: Academic Press, 1979.

Von Wright, G.H. *The Logical Problem of Induction*. New York: Oxford Press, 1957.

Wertheimer, Max. *Productive Thinking*. New York: Harper and Bros., 1959.